ESSEX FONTS
AND FONT COVERS

ESSEX FONTS AND FONT COVERS

(Norman to Nineteenth Century)

W. NORMAN PAUL F.Inst. L.Ex.

EPL

EGON PUBLISHERS LTD
Park Drive, Baldock, Herts SG7 6EW

First published in 1986
by Egon Publishers Ltd.
Park Drive, Baldock, Hertfordshire SG7 6EW

ISBN 0 905858 37 9

Designed, typeset and printed by
Streetsprinters, Park Drive, Baldock, Hertfordshire SG7 6EW
Bound by Norton Bridge, Stotfold, Hitchin, Herts.

CONTENTS

Ordnance survey references are from sheets numbered
154, 155, 167, 168, 177 and 178. 1:50000 series.

PREFACE

Those who enjoy exploring old parish churches will find much to satisfy individual tastes whether it be the intricate carving in the tracery of the screens, the carving of the effigies on sepulchral monuments, brasses or fonts of great variety, beauty and interest.

It is something for which we should be thankful, that despite the difficulties experienced by the Church in England the various parish churches have been able to preserve a priceless store of medieval art.

The earliest font in Essex is thought to be at Little Maplestead church, one of the four remaining round churches in England built by the Knights Hospitallers, and is believed to be about 1080. Apart from this font the early ones are of the twelfth century, the one at Pentlow church being richly, if crudely carved. There are, however, fonts of all periods onwards some of which are very interesting like the fifteenth century font at Bulmer church which has pagan decoration in the form of the foliate mask.

It is not only the fonts which are interesting but also the churches which are many and varied some being tucked away in isolated positions.

There are few books which deal exclusively with fonts but for those who would like to go into the study of fonts more deeply, especially those of other counties, may care to read *Fonts and Font Covers* by Francis Bond. As this book was published in 1908 it may now only be obtained through a public library or through a bookseller dealing with used books.

So far as I am aware there is not a book available which deals with Essex fonts so I have taken the opportunity to write this book which not only deals generally with fonts but also contains a survey of the fonts and font covers between the Norman period and the nineteenth century.

I have not kept strictly to the new administrative County of Essex boundaries but have included some fonts just over the boundary into the old County of Essex.

I would like to thank all those clergymen who opened up their churches for me and in many cases shared my enthusiasm and also the publishers, Egon Publishers Ltd. who have given me so much assistance.

I hope you enjoy your expeditions to Essex churches.

1986 Norman Paul

ARCHITECTURAL PERIODS

Period	Dates	Style
Saxon	600 - 1066	Romanesque
Norman	1066 - 1189	
Transitional	1145 - 1189	
Early English	1189 - 1280	Gothic
Decorated	1280 - 1377	
Perpendicular	1377 - 1547	
Early Tudor	1500 - 1547	
Late Tudor	1547 - 1603	Renaissance
Stuart	1603 - 1689	Classical
Hanoverian	1689 - 1837	

HISTORY

The Sacrament of Baptism has always ranked very highly in the Christian Church and was considered, with the Eucharist, the two Sacraments necessary for salvation and ordained by Christ Himself. Today the Sacrament of the Lord's Supper ranks higher than the Sacrament of Baptism although effort has been made to increase its importance.

The reason for the decline was that in the early days of Christianity baptism was mainly confined to adults who had been converted from the religion in which they had been born and bred to something altogether new and strange. The step was a momentous one and not without danger in the first two or three centuries of Christianity.

In the fourth century peace came to the Church and by this time it became the practice for children also to be baptised and by the eighth century had become common. For the child it was not the momentous moment in its life.

A further reason for the decline was that baptism took place only once in a person's life and then when he or she was a baby and the vows being made by proxy. For this reason the Church was unable to make much of the Sacrament of Baptism.

The Sacrament of the Eucharist was a different matter. This Sacrament was celebrated by the Church every day for many hundreds of years until the Reformation and still is in the Roman Catholic Church. It was on this Sacrament then that the Church relied to bring people to worship and a knowledge of God and so the Sacrament of the Eucharist grew in importance.

Pisa *Plate 1*

BAPTISTRY

In the early days of Christianity partial immersion in rivers was usual as can be seen in various art forms, for example, in the cubiculum of the cemetery of SS Petrus and Marcellinus, Rome, is a fresco c250 in which is a representation of the baptism of Christ showing John the Baptist laying his hand on Our Lord's head who is shown as a nude boy standing in water which is just above his ankles and again in the sixth century fresco in the baptistry of Pontranus in Rome. On a capital in Adel church, Yorkshire, and on the font in Castle Frome, Herefordshire, the water is shown rising in a heap around the waist. This was probably because the carver had insufficient space to depict the whole river and was able to represent it by piling it vertically.

Almost side by side with the practice of partial immersion there was also another usage. This was where the water flowed from above and descended on to the catechumen's head and over the whole body the catechumen standing in a vessel or shallow bath to catch the water. Representation may be seen on Greek vases where the water is shown issuing from the mouths of masks or animals.

There was also the act of affusion and in the fresco in the gallery of the sacraments in the cemetery of St. Callistus in Rome, c200 the catechumen is shown as a nude boy standing in water with water being poured on to his head by the baptiser.

Further ritual grew up comprising the triple immersion of the head in the name of the Trinity, the Father, Son and Holy Ghost. This was accomplished either by passing the head into the falling water or someone pouring water over his head three times. Whichever method was used it was not necessary to stand in a great depth of water. If the ancient tanks are examined it will be found that the maximum depth of water was about two feet and sometimes less. The shallowness of the water goes to show that the ancient form of baptism for adults was not by way of total immersion.

Baptistries were in use from early times and particularly in Italy and France where some may still be seen, for example at Pisa (plate 1) and Ravenna in Italy and at S.Jean, Poitiers. They were separate buildings and the tanks were about six or seven feet across and and about three to four feet deep (plate 2). The person to be baptised stood in about two feet of water and either immersed his head three times or water was poured over his head three times. The sacrament involved the stripping of the person, annointing with holy oil, the baptism, followed by further annointing with oil on the forehead, ears, nostrils and breast. The person was then clad in white robes representing purity and regeneration.

Now that the catechumen had been received into the Church he and any other catchumen moved into the church and joined the congregation. Baptism was the rite of initiation into the Church and the uninitiated should not enter the holy precincts until they had been admitted

Pisa *Plate 2*

through baptism (Acts 8 vs. 36-38) and so the baptistry erected for the celebration of the rite was isolated from the church; for 'baptism is the door or gate to the other sacraments and no one can participate in or be the subject of the others who has not first been baptised'.

This ceremony continued right through the Middle Ages and even when Baptism was administered at a font inside a church part of the ceremony took place in the church porch.

The size of the baptistries and the tanks was necessitated by the fact that the bishops being busy people found it necessary to restrict baptism to two or three times in the church year and there would, therefore, be a very large number of catechumens.

The next step was to stop using separate baptistries and to administer the sacrament inside the church.

When the village church obtained baptismal privileges it became usual to baptise within the church and the use of separate baptistries was brought to an end. The Council of Auxerre speaks of baptisms taking place by permission in villages as early as AD578.

In 747AD Cuthbert, Archbishop of Canterbury, ordered all priests to baptise regularly and so baptism inside the church became legalised. Pope Leo IV in the ninth century recommended that every church should have a font. It was not, of course, possible to have a font of the size that was previously used as room could not be spared and in any case by the ninth century the greater part of western Europe was nominally Christian and so adult baptism became less common.

The main reason for the change was the increasing use of infant baptism which, although not legally recognised, had been in use, to a degree, from the earliest days of Christianity.

In England a canon of the time of King Edgar, 960AD, ordered baptism of an infant not to be delayed longer than thirty-seven days. From the eleventh century onwards infants were baptised within a few days of their birth and often on the same day.

Baptism of adults had now become the exception rather than the rule with the result that the large tank was no longer necessary and so its dimensions were drastically curtailed.

Changes were also necessary in the ritual where babies were concerned. As already mentioned it was the practice for the catechumen to stand upright in shallow water but a baby could not do this and so partial submersion was substituted for the older form of semi-immersion. There are many references to this, two being contained in pontificals in the Rome Minerva Library and in the Windsor Library and are reproduced in Smith's Dictionary of Christian Antiquities.

The immersion of infants came into common use although probably not total submersion due to fears about immersing the infant's head.

Certainly in the thirteenth century S. Thomas Aquinas said that immersion was the more common form and that to be on the safe side it would be better for immersion to be practiced and not affusion, the practise of baptising by pouring water over the baby. The fifteenth century font at Gresham in Norfolk shows the baptism of a baby by immersion and it is known that Richard Beauchamp, Earl of Warwick in 1381 was baptised by immersion as were Prince Arthur, eldest son of Edward VII and Queen Elizabeth 1st. The present Book of Common Prayer of 1662 in the rubric for the Public Baptism of Infants allows for the baby or the adult to be immersed.

With the growth of infant baptism the need for the large baptismal tank ceased to exist. The font as large as was necessary for the immersion of an infant took the place of the tank and where an adult was to be baptised it would have been by affusion.

The fonts of pre-Conquest times are usually tub-shaped and were unmounted

In the eleventh and twelfth centuries unmounted fonts were less common than the mounted fonts and in the thirteenth century affusion came by degrees to be adopted and with its general use the font became smaller and more shallow and was raised from the floor on piers or columns and was termed polypod.

The older type of font continued to find favour in Italy but in the northern countries the colder climate hastened the general use of affusion and as this rite required for each person baptised only a small quantity of water the font generally took the simple form and small dimensions it has today.

In the fourteenth century fonts became tri-partite consisting of a bowl, central pedestal and base and are known as monopod.

The change from the tub font was probably brought about by convenience. When an adult was baptised it was convenient to have the tub on the floor so that he could conveniently step in and the priest could pour water over his head. With an infant, however, the priest had to stoop considerably to effect semi-immersion and as most baptisms were now of infants the font was raised on supports which were, at first, comparatively low. By the fourteenth century the practice was to mount them on a tall pedestal thus making it easier for the priest to handle the infants with greater ease.

So crucial, however, was the ceremony of baptism to Christian theology that it was natural for the pious benefactors of the later Middle Ages to make use of it architecturally. For centuries the font had been placed within the body of the nave in a position to be seen by the parishioners and where they would consider it as their responsibility and so inevitably attract their generosity.

In the fifteenth century the divinity of the font was further advanced by the elongation of the pedestal and by the number of steps, frequently three in number, leading up to the font.

The seventeenth century saw the introduction of small marble fonts in the shape of a chalice and in the eighteenth century some were vase shaped or small octagonal basins often made of marble or alabaster as at Lambourne End (117).

As almost every baby was brought to the church for baptism the priest had a close personal relationship with each family and the font was a symbol of the relationship between the priest and his congregation. It was because of this pastoral authority that ancient fonts were retained in many of our churches when the churches were re-built. An example of this is at Abbess Roding (27) where there is a late Norman font in a fourteenth century church.

MATERIALS

The font is a receptacle to hold water and derives its name from the Latin 'fons' meaning 'a spring of water' and is frequently the oldest thing in the church. Even if a church has been re-built it may never have been necessary to renew this particular feature and so a medieval font may be found in a church which has lost all trace of its medieval foundation.

Most fonts, as a rule, are made of stone lined with lead, except in those instances where the stone was impervious to water such as granite or Purbeck marble. Stone was popular in the pre-Norman period and found favour again in the fourteenth century.

The Saxon and early Norman masons cut stone with an axe which was sometimes double bladed and one can only have admiration for the results achieved.

The beginning of the Gothic period, during the last quarter of the twelfth century, saw the use of the chisel at Canterbury Cathedral although the late L. F. Salzman considered that a great deal of elaborate carving before the middle of the twelfth century must have been finished with a chisel.

There is recorded evidence that axes were used by masons down to about 1500. Nevertheless the hammer and chisel were the typical tools for dressing and carving stone.

Although Italy was the natural home of polychrome buildings English architects sometimes carried out decoration through the use of materials of contrasting colour. Strictly speaking there is no marble in England but there were a number of varieties of natural polychrome stone which was fossil limestone, a mottled black stone which, when its surface had been softened with vinegar and polished with sand appeared to catch the beauties of both marble and jasper, taking on a high polish. This fossil limestone was found at Bethersden in Kent, Petworth in Sussex and even the more widely known Purbeck 'marble'. The use of this material constitutes the most widely spread attempt at polychrome in England. The Purbeck marble was quarried in the Isle of Purbeck on the Dorset coast and was used for fonts and shafts attached to large piers or flanking doorways or windows.

The use of dark marbles for fonts and other forms of decoration was popular in the Early English period but had gone quite out of fashion by the beginning of the fourteenth century. By this time the marble work produced in the previous century had lost its original brilliant polish and masons went back to using freestone which had previously fallen out of favour.

During the Norman period Belgian marble was imported for fonts and although the origin of the Purbeck marble scheme of decoration is not certain it may be that the use of the Belgian marble suggested the decorative use of similar indiginous material.

The use of dark marble was first used in any quantity by William of Sens when he was working on Canterbury Cathedral in the twelfth century.

In the thirteenth century there was a great factory at Purbeck which produced not only marble fonts but also columns, shafts and bases. They were usually plain and simple and rarely showed originality. The fonts were usually square with shallow blank arches on each face. The arches may be pointed, trefoiled or round headed. It is difficult to understand the popularity of these factory-made fonts unless it was because they were comparatively cheap and were, perhaps, designed to have paintings in the blank arches. The polished face of the marble no doubt compensated for the lack of surface decoration. A reason for this was probably that shell marble was not a suitable material for carving intricate ornament and the risk of damage in transit was very real.

As already mentioned most fonts were made of freestone, that is stone which may be freely worked in any direction. The most successful stone being the oolite limestone, a great band of which stretches across country from Somerset through Wiltshire, Gloucestershire, Oxfordshire, Northamptonshire, Rutland, Lincolnshire to Yorkshire. The most noted quarries supplying this stone in the Middle Ages were at Barnack in Northamptonshire and Ketton in Rutland. This stone was of granular form with a gritty surface lending itself to fine carving.

One of the best freestone was the famous Caen Stone quarried in Normandy and introduced into this country by the Normans.

There are few pre-Conquest fonts extant and none in Essex. Saxon fonts were frequently made of wood and were similar to a wooden tub. They are rare and owing to their perishable nature they decayed and were replaced in stone mostly in the twelfth century. They also appear to have been considered as rather irregular. Essex has a fine example of the Perpendicular period at Marks Tey (142). It is a handsome octagonal font made of oak which in its plan of detail and ornament resembles the typical panelled stone font of the period.

Metal fonts were not prohibited but were rarely used in this country except in lead. There are only about thirty lead font bowls remaining in the country and it is thought that eight of these were cast from the same mould and belong to the twelfth or early thirteenth century. Lead fonts occurred in all periods the latest being at Aston Ingham, Herefordshire, which bears the date 1689. There are no lead bowls known in Essex.

Occasionally in the sixteenth century we find brick fonts lined with lead as at Chignal Smealey (56).

DESIGN

A very great number of Norman fonts were ornamented with blank arcading of round-headed arches, usually several arches to each face. There was also diversified ornament as well as the rich and abundant figure sculpture the subjects being mostly biblical. It is very probable that the arcading design was one submitted by the mason to the priest for approval whereas the biblical subject was proposed by the priest, the mason submitting a drawing for approval.

The thirteenth century produced little in the way of design. The Continental influence of the Romanesque had at last waned and free from Norman confines the English mason was able to work out his artistic salvation in his own way in pure Gothic. It would seem that a great share in the revolution of design was due to the masons of Purbeck. They worked in marble and the foliated capitals introduced in this century were difficult to execute in marble though this was done for Ely choir. The risk of damage to foliated ornament in course of transport to distant places was an obvious reason why masons preferred to design the fonts with as little ornament as possible other than shallow pointed arch arcading on the bowl.

Where, however, we find fonts of this period executed in freestone we find beautiful foliated design and moulded ornament which gave the period the description of 'the golden age of font design'. A good example is at Hadleigh (101).

In the fourteenth century up to the Dissolution onward a large number of fonts were re-made many of which were of simple design.

Purbeck marble became unpopular and there was a return to freestone fonts which allowed much more freedom in design.

Public opinion in the fourteenth century favoured a bowl, usually octagonal with a polygonal pedestal.

The designers were faced with the question of how to treat the normally eight faces. Previously the faces had been filled with arcading but arcading had gone out of fashion, people wanted a change. Sometimes where money was scarce the faces would be left blank. Where, however, it was possible the popular method was to ornament the faces with diversified window tracery of the day. The niche was also popular particularly when the ogee arch was used.

The designers engaged in rich and profuse ornament and the buttress was used for this purpose at each corner some terminating in crockets and finial pinnacles and some being panelled as at Chipping Ongar (59) and Chickney (55).

The tendency of the designers to copy another designer's work was prevalent in the fourteenth century but in the fifteenth century this tendency became more pronounced and there is less originality and freshness. This similarity found in fonts, particularly amongst the Seven Sacrament fonts of East Anglia, was due to copyism. One parish would arrange to have a beautiful and original font which would be greatly admired by neighbouring parishes who would arrange for a similar font to be made and so it would be copied by many parishes.

The instruments of the Passion were frequently represented on the panels of bowls for example, Thorrington (195) and Henham (107). Sometimes they occur together with shields charged with elaborate heraldry.

In the poorer parishes are found fonts with uncharged shields on the faces. These were probably meant to be painted or carved at a later date.

Fonts of this period often show traces of rich colour. It was the custom, however, of the post-Reformation churchwardens to whitewash the font or paint it sky-blue or to resemble marble.

During the nineteenth century restorations this whitewashing and daubing was scraped away, unfortunately taking with it the original painting underneath but traces of the rich gilding and colouring may often still be seen as at Harwich. (104).

LIDS AND COVERS

The very early fonts did not have lids and the christening water, having been hallowed, was kept in the font and not put in and emptied after use as it is today. One reason for this was that the hallowed water would be readily available for baptising a newly born baby without delay.

This hallowed water was considered to be of great value for black magic and witchcraft and was, therefore, sometimes stolen. To overcome these thefts various bishops throughout the country ordered that fonts should be kept locked. In 1220 the Bishop of Durham directed that fonts should be kept locked and sealed because of black magic. Edmund Rich, Archbishop of Canterbury in 1236 ordered that fonts were to be kept locked under seal and that each parish priest should hold the key of his church font because the hallowed water was used in magic. In addition it was ordered that the water was to be changed every seven days. Again in 1287 Bishop Quivel of Exeter instructed that each church in his diocese should have a well locked stone font. It is interesting that although every effort appears to have been made to protect the hallowed water in the font nothing was done in respect of the similar hallowed water in the stoup. This may have been because the font water, unlike the stoup water, had acquired something special through being sanctified to the mystical washing way of sin.

The first English Prayer Book of 1549 provided for the water to be changed once a month, the Scottish Prayer Book of 1604 required the renewal of the water every fortnight and the present Book of Common Prayer of 1662 requires that there should be a fresh supply at every baptism.

In 1305 Archbishop Winchelsey of Canterbury ordered that amongst the functions to be provided by the parishioners was a font and lock.

At first the covers were only flat lids secured by a bar and staple and it is probable that they were in general use long before the order of 1236. Many Norman fonts have holes in their rims or sides showing where the staples have been wrenched out, probably in the sixteenth century. Whether or not these fastenings were inserted prior to the order of 1236 to secure a lid, or whether they were put there as a result of the order we shall probably never know.

Not only was the font covered with a lid but between the lid and the font there was a font cloth made of linen or silk, the cloth being laid on the font and lid closed down on to it to protect the water from dust.

As the Gothic period advanced so the decorative possibilities of the font were soon appreciated and the results from the fourteenth century, developing further in the fifteenth century, especially in East Anglia, were the beautifully carved towering tabernacles of open-tracery work. One or two may be found in Essex the richest being at Takely (188) and South Weald (171).

These covers were almost always richly painted and gilded, the favourite colours being white, scarlet and green the tendency being to show increased honour to the font and which persisted for a long time after the Reformation.

In the register at Leverton church, Lincolnshire, the craftsman surveyed or viewed the font prior to carrying out the work in 1535 and the sum of four pence was given 'to karver of Boston when he came to see ye fonte' and five shillings 'to ye same for makyng a covering to the fonte'.

After the reformation in the sixteenth century when the virtues of christening water had been exploded font covers were prized away by the new Evangelists, the staples and the hinges being broken off. The scars are still be be seen.

By the middle of Queen Elizabeth's reign font covers were being destroyed and many entries may be found in church accounts and registers relating to the taking down of the font cover and yet, in some cases, a new cover was made two or three years later.

Again during the Civil War, in the seventeenth century, both fonts and covers were destroyed only to be replaced at the Restoration.

A very large number of font covers have perished for different reasons. Many Gothic covers were of highly complex and intricate design so that when they fell into disrepair it was either beyond the capabilities of the craftsmen of latter years or the pocket of the church, to carry out the necessary repairs. Often they were swept away as useless lumber at the 'restorations' of the nineteenth century.

Font covers may be divided into two kinds, those which are moveable and those which are fixed. There are four types of moveable covers (1) a flat lid which is lifted off by hand (2) an octagonal lid which is moulded on the rim and has radiating trusses rising from the angles, meeting in the centre and supporting a finial, often carved and resembling a crown as at Saffron Walden (164). Sometimes, however, they were in the shape of a pointed cone as at Roydon (162) (3) the much larger lids which varied considerably in size and weight were too heavy to lift by hand and were hung from either the roof or a beam or crane and were counterpoised with a lead, iron or stone weight as at Takely (188) and South Weald (171).

A peculiar custom following the Reformation and chiefly at the beginning of the Jacobean period was the introduction of (4) the fixed or permanent kind of covers. These enclosed the font in an ornamental wooden case which rested either permanently on the font or on the floor. The sides or lower panels hung on hinges to open when the font was required for use. Most of these disappeared in the great period of restoration when many fine fonts were brought to light. One of these ornamental cases which rested on the font may be seen at Pentlow (155) and one which rested on the floor may be seen at Thaxted (191) where the font is enclosed within wooden panelling rising to a spire-like form.

THE BAPTISMAL SERVICE

Every church was provided with a font in which infants were normally baptised on the day of their births.

The font is symbolic of regeneration through the Holy Spirit, to invest with a new and higher spiritual nature. The whole meaning of baptism is to do with re-birth and in St. John's Gospel Jesus said, 'I say unto thee except a man be born of water and of the Spirit he cannot enter into the Kingdom of God'.

To the early Chistians baptism symbolized three things. (i) Cleansing. As a person's body was cleansed by water so his soul was bathed in the mercy of Christ. (ii) Baptism marked a clean break with the past. (iii) It was a real union with Christ and as the waters closed over a person's head that person seemed to die with Christ and as the person emerged so that person rose with Christ. (Romans Ch.6 Vs. 1-4).

Fonts are usually found at the west end of the nave by the main door to indicate that baptism is the means of entrance into membership of the Church.

The medieval baptismal service was long and elaborate and in two parts, the first taking place outside the door of the church and the second at the font.

Symbolism formed a large part of the service such as exorcism of the evil spirit, the unction or anointing with spittle and oil including the putting on of the white chrisom robe which the child's mother returned when she came to be 'churched'.

The 'order for the purification of a woman after childbirth before the door of the church' describes the purpose of the rite. Scriptural authority stated that a woman who had given birth was unclean and must not 'come into the sanctuary until she had made a burnt offering and a sin offering'. The medieval service was brief consisting of a litany and Lord's Prayer, Psalms and a collect which gave thanks for deliverance from dangers of childbirth and that the woman may finish her earthly life faithfully and attain eternal life. Following this the priest sprinkled the woman with holy water and led her into church to the mass which followed. It was usual for the woman to wear a veil.

In the 1549 Book of Common Prayer the 'order for the purification of women' followed closely the medieval service. The difference was that the service was held by the chancel screen and there is no suggestion of the woman being barred from entering the church. The priest stated that the bapstism of the child had taken place and offered up thanks for safe delivery. The woman then offered back the chrisom robe given to the baby at baptism with 'other accustomed offerings' and then attended Holy Communion.

At the end of the Middle Ages, about 1500, the baptismal service was still set out in the service books in three parts, the making of a catechumen (preparation for baptism), the blessing of the font and baptism. Though virtually confined to children it still bore traces of its direct descent from the primitive rite for the baptism of adults. The first part is held at the door of the church and consists chiefly of exorcism. The priest first signs the child three times with the sign of the cross, places salt in its mouth with appropriate prayers and then adjures the devil to depart from it with further signings. The Gospel of Jesus' welcome to the children is read (Matthew 19 vs.13-15). After a charge to the godparents they join with the priest in repeating the Lord's Prayer, Hail Mary and Apostles Creed. After the final signing the child is taken into the church.

Inside the church the blessing of the font consists of a litany, a collect and a lengthy Preface exactly similar in form to that in the Mass, after which the priest pours holy oil into the water. The baptism begins with the godparents' renunciation of Satan and his 'works and pomps' after which the priest anoints the child with the 'oil of salvation'. The godparents then make their profession of faith and the child is immediately baptised by threefold immersion. It is then anointed with oil (Chrism) clothed in a white robe (Chrisom) and given a lighted candle. The parents are then charged by the priest to preserve the child from fire, water and all other dangers. The godparents are to teach the child the Lord's Prayer, Hail Mary and the Apostles Creed, to return the Chrisom and to bring the child to Confirmation as soon as the bishop comes within seven miles of the church.

Luther reduced the length of the service in 1526 by reducing the lengthy exorcism to a single appeal on oath.

Various other forms followed during the next few years.

In Cranmer's Prayer Book of 1549 he retained the two parts of the baptismal service (1) exorcism at the church door and (2) baptism at the font, but in his treatment of baptism he kept the essentials and preserved the structure while reducing the number of ceremonies and prayers and filling up the gaps with exhortations from Lutheran sources. The minister was required to dip the child in the water three times, firstly the right side, secondly the left side and thirdly dipping the face toward the font.

Cranmer's second Prayer Book in 1552 vigorously remodelled the baptismal service. Instead of the service being in two parts, one at the church door and the other at the font, the whole service took place at the font. The minister is no longer required to dip the child three times and this custom gradually fell into disuse and by 1600 affusion was general.

The superstitious ceremonies of exorcism, giving the chrisom and unction were removed together with the blessing of the font and the godparents' repetition of the Creed and Lord's Prayer. The prayers which had been used at the blessing of the font were now incorporated into the service and the questions were addressed to the godparents instead of the child. The godparents' offering not their own faith but a promise of the child's future faith. The signing of the cross was kept and the service was made to illustrate the purpose of baptism.

The 1552 Prayer Book also reflected the change in emphasis in the churching of women in that the title became 'The Thanksgiving of Women after Childbirth commonly called the Churching of Women'.

The service is now held near the 'Holy Table' and all reference to the chrisom is removed as it is no longer given in baptism.

It was the parents' obligation to have their infants baptised publicly on a Sunday or holy-day and the clergys' duty to adjure their congregations not to defer christenings longer than the first or second Sunday after birth unless for an acceptable reason. The font and no other receptacle should be used and the child should be signed with the cross by the minister.

In the Church Courts there were many cases brought against incumbents and parents for neglecting to have children baptised within the period. In 1584 a case was brought against one Edmund Binder, the incumbent of Blackmore, who was in grave trouble because 'two children died unchristened by his negligence for that he would not christen them before Sunday following and died in the meantime'. As a result Edmund Binder was suspended.

The custom of wearing a veil was frowned upon by the Puritans in the seventeenth century and many churches had special churching pews. Laudian bishops insisted on the retention of the veil and that the service should be said at the altar rail. The 1662 Book of Common Prayer laid down that the woman should 'at the usual time after her delivery . . . decently apparelled' come to church to give thanks and to offer accustomed offerings.

From the above it can be seen how Cranmer gradually refined and clarified the service of baptism, parts of which had been suggested by continental Reformers but had been rather clumsily and lengthily worded. So with little amendment the 1552 baptismal service passed into the 1662 Book of Common Prayers which is in use today and which is substantially the 1552 Prayer Book service with minor ceremonial additions.

FONTS OF VARIOUS PERIODS

PRE-CONQUEST

Fonts have existed from the ninth century onwards but it is difficult to find an example which is authentic. It has been said by some expert ecclesiologists that there are no pre-Conquest fonts extant but nevertheless there would appear to be at least twelve surviving in the country e.g. St. Martins, Canterbury, although none in Essex.

As we have many remnants of Saxon churches it is reasonable to suppose that some fonts of this period were made of stone and so being of an indestructable material, some still exist.

One reason for so few pre-conquest fonts is that although by the eleventh century every priest could baptise and every parish would have had some kind of baptismal vessel, it may have been only a stone basin or even a wooden tub which would have had a limited life and also would have been later considered as unworthy.

Another reason is that following the Conquest, in the twelfth century, most of the Anglo-Saxon churches were replaced by a Norman church and as a rule a Norman font would replace the Anglo-Saxon font.

Most were tub-shaped, often crudely carved and sometimes rudely hewn in shape although there are some finely carved pre-conquest fonts to be found in the country. A number have a band of cable ornament copied from the remains of Roman monuments of which many must have been about at that time. Others have interlacing and spiral ornament, heads and figures.

Unfortunately there are no Anglo-Saxon fonts in Essex so far as is known.

NORMAN 1066-1189

There are about thirty-seven Norman and Transitional fonts in the county both plain and enriched.

As with the buildings of the time they are solidly formed and so have withstood the intervening centuries.

The Norman fonts appear to have escaped the mutilation by the iconoclasts unlike those of later periods with their delicate carvings, traceries and figures.

The fonts of this period are generally easy to recognise because of the character of the surface decorations which in this county are mainly composed of arcading, both simple and intersecting and the sun, moon and whorl. There is very little of the typical Norman moulding, in fact the zig-zag or chevron moulding occurs only once at White Roding (214).

It is mostly the later enriched fonts which have survived like many of the enriched Norman doorways. It is possible, however, that the font at Little Maplestead (134) is early Norman circa 1080. It was not until the fifteenth century that many of the old fonts were replaced and these were generally the plainer ones and chiefly in East Anglia.

Although the shapes of the bowls vary considerably throughout the country, Essex Norman fonts are almost entirely square, or were originally, only five being circular,

Belchamp Walter (38) and Eastwood (72) being two of them. There are also four octagonal fonts of the period examples of which may be seen at Waltham Abbey (205) and Peldon (154).

There are no unmounted fonts but some were possibly originally unmounted and were mounted at a later date.

A number of fonts are polypod resting on supports of which there are normally five as at Moreton (144). Most of them are made of stone of various kinds but one or two are of Purbeck marble or have Purbeck marble supports.

The favourite form of ornamentation in the county is either the various forms of arcading i.e. round-headed arches as at Fyfield (81) or intersecting arcading made up of round-headed arches crossing each other to form pointed arches as at Eastwood (72).

The oldest font in Essex is probably that of the eleventh century at Little Maplestead (134) which has chamfered angles and raw decoration composed of a saltire cross, two arches and a composition of two volutes.

On several fonts the sun, moon and a whorl are found as at Abbess Roding (27). Foliage and petalled circles or rosettes are popular and occasionally scrolls may be found.

THIRTEENTH CENTURY – GOTHIC EARLY ENGLISH STYLE – 1189-1280

Many of the early fonts of this century and those of the late twelfth century contained a great deal of the Romanesque design of the Norman period.

It is customary, when dealing with medieval Gothic architecture to mark successive developments by special names and from the heading above it will be noted that the period is called Early English. Although these names correspond to real differences in style there are no sharp divisions between them, one style did not come to an abrupt finish and another immediately begin, one style faded gradually into another.

Architecture was a living thing and so there had to be transition as growth took place, it was a thing of continual movement. Fonts of this period may be divided into two categories (1) those made of shell marble which usually came from Purbeck in the Isle of Portland, Petworth in Sussex or Bethesden in Kent and those made of freestone but which were of the Purbeck design and (2) other freestone fonts.

The Purbeck fonts were usually square or octagonal bowls with broad flat surfaces normally resting on a central shaft with four pillars, one at each angle.

These fonts were extremely popular and to cope with the demand there was a factory at Purbeck producing ready-made shafts, moulded and floriated capitals and bases.

The change from the figure sculpture, either grotesque creatures or scenes from the Scriptures or lives of the Saints, which had been characteristic of a large class of Norman fonts went out of fashion and the ornamentation was taken almost exclusively from architectural design.

This elaborate ornamentation faded before the dazzling shine of the polished Purbeck marble.

Fonts of the second category or freestone class are less in numbers but are most interesting because of the great variety of design. The bowl is sometimes circular, square, octagonal or hexagonal as at Boreham (45). Whereas the Essex fonts of the Norman period almost all had square bowls these were giving way to octagonal bowls although square bowls were still popular.

The supports also vary, the early fonts of the period usually having detached shafts at the corners which rise to the top of the rim while the later fonts have engaged shafts at the corners supporting the base of the bowl. Some had pedestals which were often massive.

Apart from the architectural ornamentation of the period, for example, the roll moulding, the fashion of covering the surface of the font bowl with ornament was seldom adopted. Where it is to be found it takes the form of conventional foliage characteristic of the style of the period as at Springfield (172).

Bands of cable ornament and shallow arcading may also be found as at Stansted Mountfitchet (176). Some of the arcading may be pointed which we can see at West Mersea (211) or semi-circular as at Havering-atte-Bower (105) and was the most popular form of decoration.

Moulded ornament is to be found on most of the fonts and where there is foliated ornament it was used with great restraint, merely the capitals of the supports being foliated. Sometimes the water-holding moulding may be found at the base of the supports as at Ashdon (31).

The design of freestone fonts in this century was varied and very fine so that the thirteenth century may be, as Francis Bond describes it 'the golden age of font design in the comparatively few examples executed in freestone'.

Perhaps the best fonts of this period in Essex are at Newport (147) and Springfield (172). The Newport font has gabled arches in bold relief while the Springfield font has fine still-leaf foliage.

FOURTEENTH CENTURY – GOTHIC DECORATED STYLE – 1280-1377

Fonts belonging to this period, known as the Decorated period, are few in number due, no doubt, to the ample number which were provided in the Norman and Early English periods.

The design was perfected and to a large degree standardised.

The thirteenth century has been called 'the golden age of font design', now the fourteenth century may, perhaps, be called 'the brilliant age of lavish font ornament'.

Purbeck marble had gone out of fashion, not only for fonts but for shafts, capitals, bases and other items. Much of it had by this time lost much of its polish and it had begun to decay and so the masons reverted to freestone.

The fashion was to do away with the shafts whether detached or engaged and to have polygonal bowls, usually octagonal. These bowls were mounted on polygonal pedestals and were known as monopod fonts.

The simplicity of the thirteenth century had become unfashionable and in its stead rich detail was lavished on the bowls and pedestals. Perhaps some of the best is to be found in the eastern counties of Suffolk and Norfolk.

Now that the majority of bowls had eight faces it was necessary to find the best way of filling them. In the previous century arcading had provided the answer but now people were tired of it and required something different.

Where money was scarce and ornamentation could not be afforded the faces were left blank. In most cases, however, the faces were beautifully ornamented.

During this period the window tracery underwent great change and was of many patterns. Examples of window tracery were used to fill the faces of the fonts but the most popular type of filling was the niche which was used in many parts of the church, on walls, piers, tombs, sedila, screens and many other places.

There were two types which were favoured and which appeared late in the thirteenth century. One type was a straight-sided pediment, richly crocketed and cusped with a foliated finial. The other type, which was the most popular, was the new form of arch called the ogee, a form of S-shaped double curve which was greatly used until about the middle of the century when its popularity declined although it continued to be used in Gothic architecture Rayne (159).

The early niches were shallow and did not contain figures but they quickly became deeper and contained figures of saints or scriptural scenes.

Often at the corners of the base of the bowl were heads or masks, sometimes of angels or foliated ornament (Finchingfield 77). Where foliated ornament appeared it was more realistic than in the previous century and not so deeply carved.

Late in the period the pedestal tended also to be richly decorated sometimes with niches with or without figures or window tracery forms or buttresses (Willingale Spain 218).

This century has been called the Decorated period when geometrical designs were used particularly in window tracery and circular or squared quatrefoiled panels may be found round the octagonal bowl.

The cusped lancet window form and shields were favourite ornaments (Great Saling 94).

Figure sculpture which was common on Norman fonts, but was rarely used in the thirteenth century, reappears and is much more lifelike than the grotesque figures of the Normans. In Essex it takes the form of human heads or masks as at Finchingfield (77).

The splendid architecture of the Decorated period was reaching its apogee when it was suddenly halted by the terrible pestilence known as the Black Death which broke out in south-west England in 1348.

The plague swept through the country and by 1349 had become so widespread that the consequent mortality paralysed the country. It is estimated that about one half of the population perished.

Building operations practically came to a stop due to the scarcity of masons and in 1350 when the great re-building of Gloucester Cathedral was finished the surviving masons and others were organised and sent out into various parts of the country which probably accounts for the standardisation of architecture from about the last quarter of the century.

The monasteries were very badly hit and became depleted with the result that religious life deteriorated and so no great abbeys were built in the fifteenth century and the new Perpendicular style quickly found its way into parish churches.

FIFTEENTH CENTURY – GOTHIC PERPENDICULAR STYLE – 1377-1547

As a result of the plague religion appears to have become generally more devotional and guilds and chantries multiplied.

This period tended to become the setting for the work of craftsmen in glass, sculpture and wood carving and so we find that their skill is directed especially to church furnishings and ornaments making this period the apogee of church fittings and furniture.

Many of our finest churches were built in this period by the great wool and cloth merchants as for example Saffron Walden church.

As previously mentioned Gothic architecture was a thing of continual movement but in the Perpendicular period, which lasted some one hundred and seventy years or thereabouts, it began to show signs of deterioration. In the best work there must be progress, once the movement ceases then development fails and in the Perpendicular period it slowed down and began to come to rest and so with the ceasing of the movement deterioration set in.

In the Early English and Decorated periods there was feeling about the architecture and furnishings, the carving was vigorous and natural. In this period, however, everything showed that skill and dexterity were the things after which the craftsmen were striving.

One sign of this deterioration was the repetition of forms of ornament and yet despite this the period had many deserving qualities. Their timber and vaulted roofs which were gloried in by the carpenters, wood-carvers and masons, the screens, canopy work, stalls and misericords, pulpits and fonts as well as parts of the fabric were clothed with miniature buttresses, pinnacles, vaults and battlements.

With so much attention being given to the furnishings of the church the font was very much included and the number of Perpendicular fonts far exceed those of any period since the Norman.

The octagonal form of bowl was now usually employed.

Some fonts had little ornament but many had quatrefoil and heraldic ornament with shields on the sides of the bowls bearing the arms of donors or benefactors, examples of which may be seen at North Fambridge (149) and Shalford (167). Rosettes and fleurettes were also a popular form of decoration.

The most popular type which one might say is a typical Perpendicular font has the sides panelled. In each panel is a quatrefoil or a quatrefoil within a circle as at Southminster (170). In many instances the stem is also ornamented with panel tracery.

A local type to be found in Essex has an octagonal bowl with the faces concave in form, examples of which may be seen at Ashingdon (33), North Fambridge (149) and Prittlewell (156).

During this period brick was coming into general use and was often used in church architecture in the eastern counties. In a few cases, where the church was built of brick, this material was also used for the font as at Chignal Smealey (56).

Figure sculpture which had been prevalent in the Norman period and which had comprised human or animal figures, was revived. The figures on Perpendicular fonts generally represent saints and angels and are more realistic and life-like than the grotesque figures of the Norman period, East Mersea (70).

A further feature of this period is the traceried pedestal which appears on a large number of Essex fonts as at High Laver (110).

Wooden fonts are rare but at Marks Tey (142) is a fine octagonal font made of oak with ornament resembling a typical panelled font of the fifteenth century.

FONTS WITH PROJECTIONS

As already mentioned S. Thomas Aquinas made it clear in the thirteenth century that immersion was to be preferred to affusion as more properly representing death to sin but that affusion was to be regarded as valid. When an infant was baptised by immersion the hallowed water in which it had been immersed was used again and again and it was not surprising, therefore, that there was repugnance over the continued repetition of baptism over a font in which the water had not been changed for many weeks. To overcome this a way was found by providing two compartments by way of a stone or lead partition. One division was filled with hallowed water and the child was held over the other division so that the drippings might fall into the dry portion of the bowl from which they were conveyed away by a drain.

Much later in 1614 Pope Paul V issued a series of instructions in the Rituale Romanum and under the heading 'De Forma Baptisme' was the following exhortation. 'The water from the child's head is not to be allowed to drip into the font. Either it is to drip into a piscina built adjoining the font or it is to be caught in some vessel provided for the purpose and poured into a piscina near the font or in some ofther piscina in the church'.
This instruction would be satisfied by the partitioned bowl as described.

Fonts are to be found having projections which have given rise to a diversity of explanations as to their use most of which are unsound.

The projections are various, for example, a small rounded basin or stoup almost level with the rim, a bracket-like projection or a number of bracket-like projections.

The small rounded basin, if it contained a drain, could have been used to catch the drips from the child's head or alternatively, if there was no drain, could have held a basin which, after the baptism, could have been emptied in the churchyard or into a nearby piscina.

In the Middle Ages from the thirteenth century onwards baptism by aspersion, that is where the holy water was sprinkled on the head, was practiced as well as affusion and it gradually became more common. Aspersion had been permitted from the earliest times but usually only in the case of necessity. Pope Clement V formally recognised the practice in 1305 and in the fifteenth century Lyndewood declared that 'it is sufficient that a small drop of water thrown by the baptizer touch him who is to be baptised. It is sufficient that water which has been sprinkled touch some part of the body'.

It would seem that England did not readily disregard the ancient practice of immersion so early as the Continental churches. According to Erasmus, an eminent Dutch theologian (1467-1536), he noted that in England infants were still immersed and sprinkling did not become general till after the Reformation.

The projecting brackets, where they had a flat surface, probably held the affusion bowl and where there was more than one bracket, perhaps the salt and candle. At Rainham (157) there is a circular Norman font on one side of which there is a semi-circular projection level with the rim whilst on the opposite side is a small portion of another similar projection most of which is broken away.

Some of the brackets have holes in the surface and it is probable that where this is found the brackets served as supports for the hinges of a heavy font cover or perhaps to hold a shelf on which the bowl could be placed.

It would seem that the practice of catching the drips from the child's head was still in vogue in the eighteenth century and at Essendon, Herts, we find a Wedgwood bowl in which there used to be a small gilt basin which, when not in use was placed on a small wooden support on the floor but at a baptism was placed inside the Wedgewood bowl. The small basin would have been used for affusion or aspersion and the bowl to catch the drips.

From early times and throughout the Middle Ages the method of pouring water over the head of the catechumen who was immersed in the water was by way of a shallow bowl. On the south door of the baptistry of Florence Cathedral is a bronze bas-relief showing St. John-the-Baptist baptising in the wilderness using a shallow bowl (plate 3).

On a cross at Kells, County Meath, Ireland, can be seen a spoon used for affusion and on some of the fifteenth and sixteenth century Seven-Sacrament fonts in East Anglia a jug was used as at Gresham and Stalham in Norfolk.

When immersion ceased and affusion only was practised in Europe the Synod of Aix in 1585 ordered that 'the pouring of water be not done with the hand but with a ladle kept in the font for that purpose'. Today a shell is sometimes used.

Florence *Plate 3*

POST-REFORMATION FONTS

Several years elapsed before the religious changes brought about by the Reformation affected the font and there were few new fonts between the reign of Elizabeth and the Civil War.

In Queen Elizabeth's reign those who had been exiled on the continent during the persecutiion of Mary's reign returned to this country but could not accept the sacramental system and ceremonial of the English Church.

The performance of Divine worship and the celebration of the rites of the Church were beset with confusion and carelessness and the Church authorities found it difficult to bring decency and order to bear.

The Calvanistic custom of baptising in basins grew and Injunctions and Visitation Articles contained references to it in an attempt to check the spread of this custom. By royal command Injunctions were issued under the name of Queen Elizabeth 'that the font be not removed from the accustomed place; and that in parish churches the curates take not upon them to confer baptism in basins but in the font customably used'. Despite this Injunction destruction of fonts and negligent administration grew and there are many instances of demolition recorded in churchwardens' accounts where parishes defied the royal orders.

During the Civil War some fonts were destroyed but it was not until the Commonwealth when the Puritans had gained the ascendancy that the use of fonts was expressly forbidden and there was wholesale destruction. Many instances occurred where the carved font panels were plastered over to make them appear to be plain and uncarved only to be re-discovered some centuries later. This disguising of some fonts saved them from destruction when the inspectors made their visits. The font at Belchamp St. Paul (37) has two of its panels plastered over and as the decoration is in such good condition it is very probable that all the panels were dealt with accordingly so saving it from destruction. The font at Great Maplestead (91) was completely plastered and painted. The plaster was removed in 1930 and traces of the paint may still be seen.

With the Restoration new fonts were put up to replace those which had been destroyed.

In 1662 the Act of Uniformity was passed by which no one could hold a living who had not declared his unfeigned assent and consent to everything therein. This meant that basins were not to be used and fonts were to be brought back into use.

The many parishes which had destroyed their fonts now had to have new fonts or where only the bowls had been destroyed then new bowls were mounted on the old pedestals.

Occasionally the old font was not always destroyed but hidden away and brought out for re-erection.

During the popularity of the Neo-Classical style following on the work of Inigo Jones and Sir Christopher Wren fonts conformed to the new fashion taking the form of vases and bowls on pillars. Sometimes the bowls of fonts of this style were decorated with miniature cherubs heads which became popular as an adornment to various items of church furnishings. The font at Billericay (39) is a good example of this style.

Alphabetical List and Description of Fonts

ST. EDMUND ABBESS RODING

Church Foundation: Fourteenth century

Polypod. Square bowl. Norman. Late twelfth century.

Decoration

South face: Star enclosing rosette, one at each end. Whorl, moon and sun in centre.
East face: Two six-petalled circles, one at each end with three small rosettes in centre of face.
North face: Trails of foliage.
West face: Trails of foliage, possibly vine.
The square bowl is very damaged but has been partly repaired with bands of iron and inserts across the cracks.
The bowl is mounted on a short central round pedestal and four slender shafts at the angles. This is all modern.
The base looks much older and the whole is mounted on a square sub-base with priest's step.
In 1638 the Archdeacon ordered the font to be painted to obliterate the carvings and traces of green paint may still be seen.

O.S. Ref. No. 572 114

ST. BARNABAS (1975) (ORIGINAL DEDICATION LOST) — ALPHAMSTONE

Church Foundation: Norman

Monopod. Square bowl. Purbeck type. Purbeck marble. Norman, twelfth century.

Decoration

The large square bowl has shallow blank arcading comprising five round-headed arches to each side. The underside is chamfered to pedestal.
The rim is damaged where lid fastenings have been removed.
The circular pedestal has two half-round mouldings at the top the lower half spreading out to a square stepped base.
At some time the font has been covered with a layer of plaster which was removed in 1902 when the chancel was restored.

Cover

The octagonal boarded and ribbed semi-globe shaped cover is made of oak crowned by a finial of openwork scrolls fixed to a central baluster terminating in a turned ball. It is obvious that the cover was not made for this font.

O.S. Ref. No. 879 354

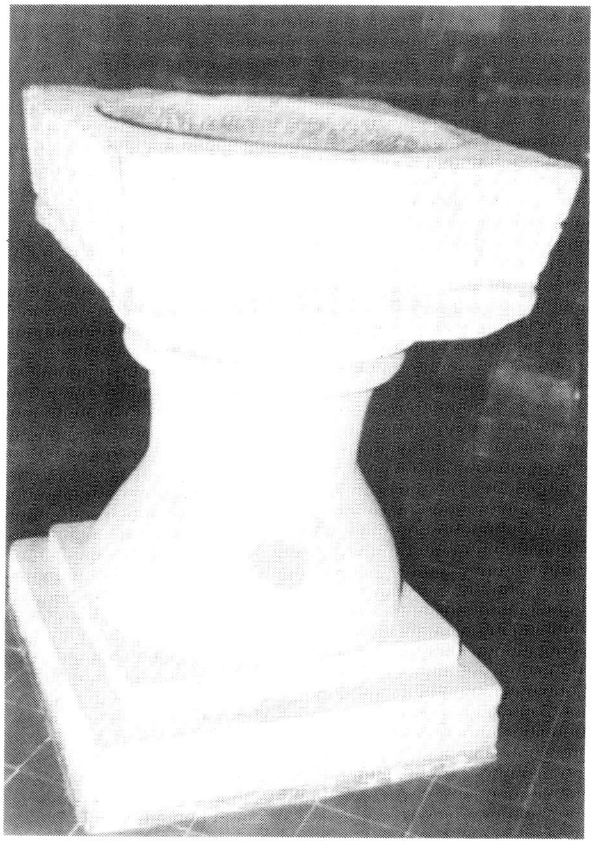

ST. ANDREW ALTHORNE

Church Foundation: Perpendicular.

Monopod. Octagonal bowl. Perpendicular c. 1400.

Decoration

This font is one of the finest in Essex. The octagonal bowl has deeply carved recessed panels which record the costumes worn by kings and queens and ordinary people of that age and throw the figures into strong relief. Although the carving cannot be said to be good it is vigorous.

East face: Seraph covered with feathers.
North-east face: King and Queen.
North face: Man and Woman.
North-west face: Baptism of a Royal Prince.
West face: Blank. It would seem that the carving has been chiselled away. Was it originally a crucifix?
South-west face: Figures of two men.
South face: Martyrdom of St. Andrew.
South-east face: Two men with scrolls.

The lower edge of each panel is embattled and the underneath of the bowl is chamfered to pedestal. On the chamfer are carved winged angels at each angle. Each face of the octagonal pedestal has a deeply recessed trefoiled head window form in the upper part divided by moulding from a pointed-lobed quatrefoil with fleuron in centre.

The octagonal base has a moulded top edge and on each face there are two fleurons.

The whole now stands on the monumental floor slab of Elizabeth Gordon.

O.S. Ref. No. 909 989.

ST. MARY THE VIRGIN — ARKESDEN

Church Foundation: Early English (built on site of earlier church).

Polypod. Square tapered bowl. Barnack stone. (Originally unmounted.) Norman, twelfth century.

Decoration

The twelfth century square bowl is tapered to supports being divided by a fillet moulding.
The supports are thirteenth century and are unusual being constructed as a solid base with through pointed arches on each side thus forming square corner supports. The arches and responds have hollow chamfer and half-round mouldings.
The whole is mounted on a square base which has had a priest's step added.

Cover

The flat wooden cover is modern heavily covered with decorative wrought iron.

O.S. Ref. No. 482 346

ALL SAINTS ASHDON

Church Foundation: Decorated (probably adapted from a previous Saxon or Norman church)

Monopod. Irregular octagonal bowl. Early English, early thirteenth century (perhaps earlier).

Decoration

The faces are plain and irregular in size which would appear to be evidence that the bowl was originally square and later re-cut when it was rebuilt on to the present pedestal.

The octagonal pedestal has a moulded top and bottom and is probably very early fourteenth century.

The base is square with chamfered edge with priest's step.

The font is not in its original position probably having been moved from the west end of the south aisle.

Cover

The attractive octagonal wooden boarded cover is late seventeenth century. It is trumpet-shaped with vertical sided base moulded on top and bottom edges, the sides having a band of carved work on each face. The concave ribs terminate in a small flat moulded base containing a Latin cross finial.

The cover is painted in green and yellow and some of the faces have paintings of lilies. The painting was possibly a nineteenth century addition.

O.S. Ref. No. 581 415

ST. AUGUSTINE OF CANTERBURY — ASHEN

Church Foundation: Early English (Site of Saxon or Norman church).

(Original dedication unknown but known as St. Augustine since 1853).

Monopod. Octagonal bowl. Decorated, fourteenth century.

Decoration

The small octagonal bowl has plain faces and is chamfered on the lower edge. The high octagonal pedestal and base with chamfered top edge are much later than the bowl.
Originally the bowl was beautifully carved and dates from c.1390.
Between 1649 and 1660 the carving was cut off and the base smashed to pieces and buried. In 1857 when excavations were carried out in the churchyard the broken pieces were discovered and re-buried.

O.S. Ref. No. 744 423.

ST. ANDREW ASHINGDON

Church Foundation: Saxon.

Monopod. Octagonal bowl. Early Tudor, early sixteenth century.

Decoration

The octagonal bowl is similar to the Faulkbourne and Prittlewell fonts in having plain concave faces.
The underside of the bowl has stepped hollow-chamfers to octagonal pedestal which has slightly concave sides.
The top of the base has hollow-chamfered concave sides with a deep quirk under to vertical concave sides.
The rim of the bowl contains marks of lid fastenings.
The font has been painted and some of the paint remains.

Cover

The cover is a flat octagonal wooden lid with chamfered edge on top of which is a wrought iron equal armed cross each arm terminating with a fleur-de-lis. In the centre is a cable ring handle. Modern.

O.S. Ref. No. 866 936

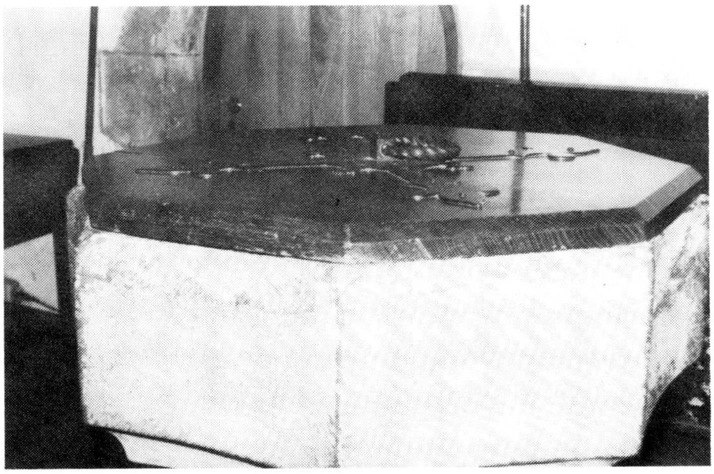

ST. MICHAEL AVELEY

Church Foundation: Norman.

Polypod. Square bowl. Purbeck marble. Norman, twelfth century.

Decoration

Each face has four shallow blank round-headed arches.
The bowl is badly cracked and worn and the rim shows marks of lid fastenings.
The bowl is mounted on a plain round pedestal and four plain round angle shafts on a square base. The whole is mounted on a square sub-base with priest's step.

Cover

The cover is a flat octagonal wooden lid with chamfered moulded edge.
In the centre is a smaller flat octagonal base with chamfered moulded edge rising from which is a turned baluster central shaft with four open ogee trusses each carved on the outside face with an acanthus leaf. The central shaft ends with a small flat octagonal with orb finial. Modern 1956.

O.S. Ref. No. 568 801

ST. PETER AND ST. PAUL — BARDFIELD SALING

Church Foundation: Early perpendicular

Monopod. Octagonal bowl. Perpendicular, late fourteenth century. (1380).

Decoration

The rim of the octagonal bowl has been damaged by the removal of the lid fastenings but has been repaired. The rim edge is chamfered with a quirk under.
Each face has a recessed ogee arch.
The underside of the bowl is stepped with a hollow-chamfer to the pedestal.
The octagonal pedestal has a plain recessed pointed arch on each face.
The small base is octagonal with chamfered top edge.
The whole is mounted on a square sub-base with priest's step.

Cover

The cover is a plain wooden lid with an equal armed iron cross with cable ring handle.
This church was originally a chapel-of-ease for Great Bardfield church.

O.S. Ref. No. 686 265

ALL SAINTS BARLING

Church Foundation: Norman.

Monopod. Octagonal bowl. Perpendicular, fifteenth century.

Decoration

The octagonal font has panelled faces. The rim is moulded and is damaged in various places.
East face: uncharged shield in relief.
North-east face: Uncharged shield in relief.
North face: This face is against a pillar and is plain.
North-west face: Uncharged shield in relief.
West face: Uncharged shield in relief.
South-west face: Recessed round-lobed quatrefoil within a circle.
South face: Recessed round-lobed quatrefoil within a circle.
South-east face: Recessed round-lobed quatrefoil within a circle.
The underside of the bowl is moulded.
The pedestal is octagonal having a buttress with two set-offs at each angle.
The base is octagonal with chamfered top edge and vertical sides.
The whole is mounted on a seven sided sub-base against a pillar.

Cover

The cover is a flat oak lid with moulded edge. In the centre is a square stop-chamfered post having a moulded base. From alternate faces of the lid rise four convex trusses cusped on the inside and meeting at the top of the central post which terminates in a patée cross. Modern.

O.S. Ref. No. 933 897.

ST. ANDREW — BELCHAMP-ST.-PAUL

Church Foundation: Perpendicular (probably on site of Norman church).

Monopod. Octagonal bowl. Perpendicular, fifteenth century.

Decoration

East face: Uncharged shield within pointed-lobed quatrefoil.
North-east face: Fleurette within pointed-lobed quatrefoil having a peardrop shape in each lobe.
North face: Uncharged shield within pointed-lobed quatrefoil.
North-west face: Diagonal cross in square.
West face: Blank.
South-west face: Blank.
South face: Small plain disc in centre of pointed-lobed quatrefoil.
South-east face: Diagonal cross in square.
Bottom of bowl chamfered to fine mouldings.
Stem plain octagonal with fine mouldings to hollow chamfer at base. The whole mounted on shallow octagonal step.
It is difficult to account for the two blank faces but it would appear that the recesses have been filled at some time to obliterate the carving, perhaps during Puritan times, although it seems odd that they have not been restored by now. On the other hand the font could have originally been in a corner.
From an examination of the stonework it would appear that the bowl has been remounted.

Cover

Flat octagonal wooden cover with octagonal moulded knob. Modern.

O.S. Ref. No. 798 435.

ST. MARY — BELCHAMP WALTER

Church Foundation: Early English (probably on site of Norman Church).

Originally unmounted. Circular with straight sides. Norman, twelfth century (early). Probably from earlier church.

Decoration

The rim of the large bowl is damaged and it would appear that the original top has been removed thus spoiling the carved decoration. The carving is composed of beaded scrolls, vine leaves and acanthus leaves. Just below the carving is a quirk running round the bowl.

The bowl is now mounted on a round base with half-round moulding. The whole is mounted on a stepped square step.

Cover

The flat circular wooden cover is surmounted with a wooden cross. Modern.

O.S. Ref. No. 827 407

ST. MARY MAGDALENE BILLERICAY

Church Foundation: Perpendicular.

Monopod. Round bowl. Classical, eighteenth century.

Decoration

The small round bowl, resembling a flower vase rather than the traditional form of font, has a moulded edge which is damaged. From the rim project two cherubs heads and the bottom of the bowl is decorated with a form of gadroon moulding.

The bowl stands on a slender pedestal with moulded top and hollow moulding. The centre and lower parts resemble an inverted mushroom under which the small moulded base stands on a rectangular sub-base which has two cut-off corners.

Cover

The cover is a round wooden lid with egg and dart moulding on edge of rim with a raised moulded circular disc the centre containing a Latin cross. Modern.

O.S. Ref. No. 674 946

ST. MARY BIRCHANGER

Church Foundation: Norman.

Monopod. Octagonal bowl. Perpendicular, fifteenth century.

Decoration

Each face of the bowl is plain but covered with graffiti.
Lower edge is moulded.
The stem is octagonal having three trefoil headed lancets on each face.
Mounted on plain octagonal base.

O.S. Ref. 507 227

ST. AUGUSTINE OF CANTERBURY BIRDBROOK

Church Foundation: Norman.

Monopod. Octagonal bowl. Eighteenth century (1791) (Gothic imitation).

Decoration:

The small bowl is octagonal with a hollow-chamfered edge to the rim.
The underside of the bowl is moulded and hollow-chamfered to the pedestal.
The faces are recessed and panelled.
East face: Miniature painting representating 'The Baptism of Christ' within a round-lobed quatrefoil. It is suggested by Pevsner that the painting is by the seventeenth century artist Samuel Cooper (1609-1672) in which case it is about a century earlier than the font.
North-east face: Round-lobed quatrefoil with fleurette in centre.
North face: Pointed-lobed octfoil containing a five pointed star.
North-west face: Charged shield.
West-face: A crown with a stylised feather rising from centre.
South-west face: Round-lobed quatrefoil with fleurette in centre.
South face: Pointed-lobed octfoil containing a five pointed star.
South-east face: Agnes Dei.
Around the rim are the words 'The gift of Thomas Walford Esq. of Whiteleys 1791'. The church guide book states that this font replaced the old font in 1763.
The underside of the bowl is moulded and hollow-chamfered.
Each face of the pedestal has a recessed trefoiled head window form. The bottom of the pedestal is moulded above an octagonal straight-sided plain base.

The whole is mounted on an octagonal straight-sided sub-base with priest's step.

Cover

The cover is a flat octagonal wooden lid with moulded edge which bears eight concave crocketed open ribs carved with a leaf design. Between some of the ribs, on top of the lid, are the remains of open-leaf fret.

The ribs which are painted white rise to an octagonal cap just below a gold painted patée cross.

O.S. Ref. No. 721 388

ST. LAWRENCE BLACKMORE

Church Foundation: Norman.

Monopod. Octagonal bowl, Purbeck marble. Early English, thirteenth century.

Decoration

All faces plain. (May have had some shallow decoration at some time). Very worn.
Octagonal stem having plain faces mounted on octagonal base with chamfered upper edge.
Single step with priest's stone.

O.S. Ref. 604 017

ST. PETER AND ST. PAUL BLACK NOTLEY

Church Foundation: Norman.

Monopod. Octagonal bowl. Perpendicular style, fifteenth century.

Decoration

Each face is panelled and contains a round-lobed quatrefoil with fleurette in centre.
Part of underside of bowl is moulded the lower part being decorated with vine leaves and grapes.
The pedestal is octagonal with plain sides but having very nice moulding at its base. It is mounted on an octagonal base on which are carved the letters P.C. AD 1806.

This font is a copy of the original font in this church.

O.S. Ref. No. 762 207

ST. GERMAN'S BOBBINGWORTH

Church Foundation: Early English

Monopod. Octagonal bowl. Perpendicular, fifteenth century.

Decoration

Each face of the octagonal bowl is plain.

The bowl stands on an octagonal pedestal having a moulded top with an octagonal base which has the top edge hollow chamfered. The font has been badly damaged and is cracked around the bowl. There is also a large piece of stone missing from the rim of the west face probably caused by wrenching away the lid fastening on that side. On the rim of the east face are the remains of the other part of the lid fastening in its original lead setting.

The south-east face contains graffiti in the form of the letters JP but nothing is known as to what they represent. Probably someone doodling. The font is made up of two parts, the bowl and the pedestal. It is said that the bowl was used as a flower bowl in Nettleswell church for one hundred years but was recognised as having come from a church and so was placed in the churchyard of Little Parndon. A former rector of Bobbingworth, Canon Gallop, discovered the bowl in Little Parndon churchyard and brought it back to find that it fitted on to the existing old Bobbingworth pedestal on which a nineteenth century bowl stood. The old bowl has now been placed on the old pedestal. There is little doubt that although the bowl fits the old pedestal they do not appear to be compatible. In addition the stone used for the bowl is not the same as that used for the pedestal. The whole stands on a modern sub-base.

O.S. Ref. No. 535 056

ST. ANDREW — BOREHAM

Church Foundation: Saxon.

Unmounted, tub. Hexagonal bowl, Clunch. Decorated, late thirteenth century.

Decoration

The hexagonal bowl has a moulded rim and is straight sided.
Each side has a gabled blank trefoiled head arch. The backs of the trefoiled arches are faced with Victorian tiles.
The lower edge is moulded and the whole is set on an hexagonal base having its top edge chamfered.

O.S. Ref. 756 096

ST. MARGARET BOWERS GIFFORD

Church Foundation: Decorated.

Monopod. Octagonal bowl. Perpendicular, c1500.

Decoration

The octagonal bowl has plain faces with hollow-chamfer and moulding underneath.
The rim is damaged but contains parts of the lid fixing staples.
The short plain octagonal pedestal has an octagonal base with chamfered top.

Cover, c1600

The cover is composed of an octagonal flat wooden lid with moulded edge. From the lid rises a plain boarded cone with plain ribs at each angle to a finial decorated with lozenge patterns. Probably made by local carpenter. The cover retains traces of colouring and has been repaired.

O.S. Ref. No. 756 873

ST. LAWRENCE BRADFIELD

Church Foundation: Early English.

Polypod. Octagonal bowl. Early English, thirteenth century.

Decoration

The octagonal bowl is slightly tapered. There are remains of lid fastenings in the rim and in the south-east face of the bowl.

Each face has two shallow blank pointed arches which have been crudely carved.

The angle between the north-east and north faces is well out of true. Is it possible that the bowl is older than the thirteenth century and was originally square, later being re-cut by a local craftsman in the thirteenth century to make it more 'modern'.

The font has been re-mounted the pedestal and one of the supporting shafts having been renewed but seven of the eight shafts are original.

The shallow octagonal base is modern having a chamfered top edge the whole being mounted on a deep octagonal sub-base.

The font was previously close to the west door but was moved at the beginning of the century to a point further to the south.

O.S. Ref. No. 144 308

HOLY TRINITY BRADWELL-JUXTA-COGGESHALL

Church Foundation: Norman.

Monopod. Octagonal bowl. Norman, twelfth century.

Decoration

The bowl was originally square but in the early seventeenth century it was re-shaped into eight sides and set up on an elaborate brick base.
The rim edge has pellet moulding in those parts of the original faces.
East, north and west faces have chevron moulding but the south face is indistinguishable. The remaining faces are plain.
The brick seventeenth century base has a moulded brick top. Underneath each face has a pierced round-headed quatrefoil with half-round moulded brick under. The brickwork is then formed into a hollow-chamfer to the octagonal base.

Cover

The wooden cover is Jacobean c1700, octagonal and raised up above the font. The top is boarded and from the boarded top rises a truncated panelled cone with moulded too and culminating in a ball finial. The cover is hoisted by rope and pulley.

O.S. Ref. No. 818 222

ST. THOMAS-THE-APOSTLE BRADWELL-JUXTA-MARE

Church Foundation: Decorated.

Monopod. Octagonal bowl. Decorated, fourteenth century.

Decoration

The octagonal bowl is damaged and repaired in places.
The faces on the north-east, north-west, south-west and south-east are plain.
The east, north, west, and south faces have large heads at the bottom and extending to the pedestal through moulding on underside of the bowl. They seem as though their shoulders are bearing the weight of the bowl.
North head: protruding tongue.
East head: woman's head.
South head: tonsored.
West head: has jewelled circlet.
The large stone base is octagonal with chamfered top edge.

Cover

The cover is a flat stepped wooden lid with an iron cross having trefoiled arms and a central ring handle.

O.S. Ref. No. 004 069

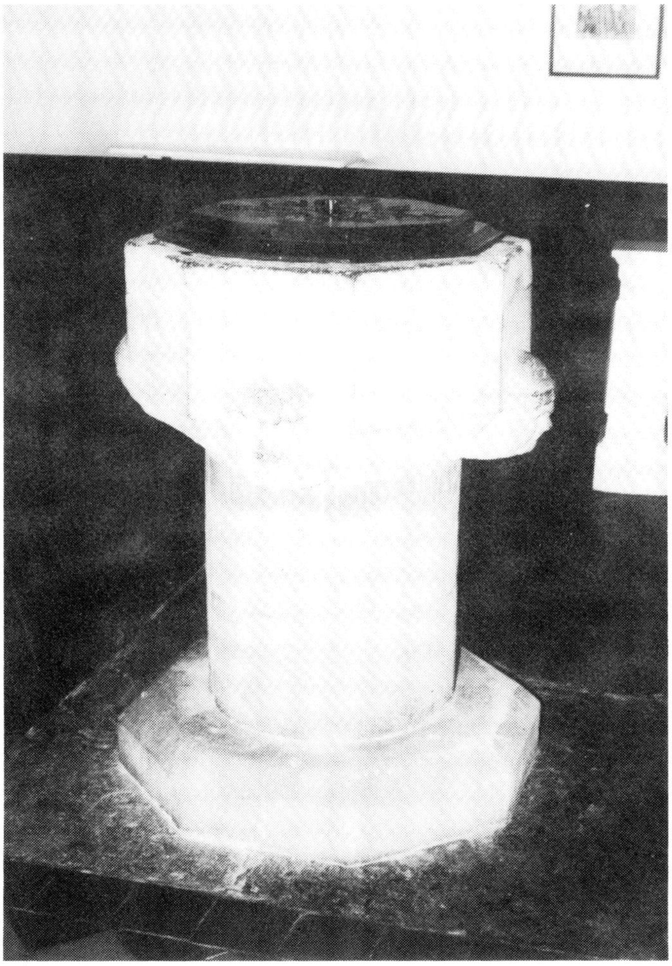

ALL SAINTS BRIGHTLINGSEA

Church Foundation: Norman (overlies a Roman Villa)

Monopod. Octagonal bowl. Perpendicular, fifteenth century.

Decoration

The octagonal bowl has a recessed pointed-lobed quatrefoil enclosing a rose on each face. The east and south-east roses are mounted on square blocks. The bowl has been damaged but repaired.

There are remains of lid fastenings in the rim.

The underside of the bowl is moulded and hollow-chamfered to the top of the pedestal. On each face of the chamfer is a square fleuron.

The short octagonal pedestal has a recessed window form with cinquefoiled head on each face.

The vertical sides of the base are plain the top edges being hollow-chamfered and would not appear to be original.

There is a substantial amount of colouring remaining on the bowl and pedestal.

The whole is mounted on an octagonal sub-base with priest's step.

Cover

The cover is an octagonal cone rising from vertical sides each having three pierced round-headed quatrefoils with floriated cusps within circles. The cone is ribbed and boarded each rib having five crockets and rising to a foliated finial which is damaged.

The cover is raised by two wires, over pulleys, the wires being fixed to metal cylinder weights.

O.S. Ref. No. 087 168

ST. MARY BROOMFIELD

Church Foundation: Norman.

Polypod. Square bowl, Purbeck marble. Early English, thriteenth century (transitional).

Decoration

Each of the four sides has three shallow blank pointed arches and an unusual feature, attached columns with stiff leaf capitals and water-holding moulded bases at the angles.

The bowl is mounted on a drum pedestal (modern) and four unattached angle shafts having scalloped capitals and roll moulded bases. These angle shafts are doubtful, they may be original but in 1856 the font bowl was relegated to a spare corner and not used a modern substitute having taken its place. There did not appear to be any shafts or pedestal at that time.

The bowl is well worn and parts of the hasp and staple lid fastenings are still in situ.

The whole is mounted on a rectangular sub-base with priest's step.

Cover

The cover is a square flat wooden lid with an equal armed iron fimbriated patonée cross and central ring handle. Modern.

O.S. Ref. No. 705 105

ST. ANDREW BULMER

Church Foundation. Decorated.

Monopod. Octagonal bowl. Perpendicular, fifteenth century.

Decoration

This font is beautifully carved and preserved. The rim is unusually moulded with round and square type billet moulding.
East face: Green Man (fertility symbol).
North-east face: Open winged angel holding uncharged shield.
North face: Vine leaf in each corner with seven petalled rosette in centre.
North-west face: Open winged angel holding uncharged shield.
West face: Vine leaf in each corner with seven petalled rosette in centre.
South-west face: Open winged angel holding uncharged shield.
South face: Pointed-lobed quatrefoil containing charged shield. First and third quarters charged with what may be a thumb-screw and second and fourth quarters with a series of cusps.
South-east face: Open winged angle holding an uncharged shield which has been repaired.
The rim of the bowl shows marks where lid fastenings have been removed.
The bowl is cracked and repaired on the south-east face.
Underside edge of bowl is moulded with a fleurette on each face.
The stem is octagonal and on each face there is a traceried window formation consisting of two trefoiled head lancets with two more underneath divided by a transom.

The base of the stem is stepped with two rows of hollow chamfers on a small octagonal base with separate priest's step.

O.S. Ref. No. 843 402

ST. MARY — BURNHAM-ON-CROUCH

Church Foundation: Decorated (on site of previous church)

Polypod. Square bowl, Purbeck marble. Norman, late twelfth century

Decoration

The square bowl is roughly hewn and has plain sides.
The bowl is mounted on a drum pedestal with four engaged round corner shafts.
The whole is mounted on a stepped square base the top edge of the lower step being chamfered.

Cover

The cover is a square flat lid with rounded edge and chamfered corners. In the centre is a square baluster to which are fixed four concave pierced trusses. The central baluster terminates in a bulb finial. Modern.

O.S. Ref. No. 949 971

ST. NICHOLAS CANEWDON

Church Foundation: Decorated (there was a Norman church on this site)

Polypod. Square bowl. Early English, early thirteenth century.

Decoration

East face: Three blank trefoiled arches the centre arch having foliated cusps.
South face: Intersected round-headed blank arcading with piers having finely moulded capitals and bases.
The north and west faces appear to be blank although Pevsner says that they have fleur-de-lis and crosses in niches.
The rim of the bowl worn and partly damaged.
The bowl rests on a central pedestal with half-round moulding and four detached corner shafts each having Early English capitals and bases (water holding moulding). The shafts have been badly repaired.

The small square base is single stepped.

This font was transferred from the demolished church at Shopland in 1957.

O.S. Ref. No. 896 945.

ST. MARY — CHICKNEY

Church Foundation: Saxon.

Polypod. Octagonal bowl, Clunch (local name for chalk limestone). Perpendicular, early fifteenth century.

Decoration

East face: Small charged shield (Braybrook arms).
North-east face: Small uncharged shield.
North face: Small uncharged shield.
North-west face: Small uncharged shield.
West face: Small uncharged shield.
South-west face: Small uncharged shield.
South face: Small charged shield (Fitzwalter arms).
South-east face: Small charged shield (Unidentified).
Octagonal central stem on square base with chamfered corners.
Four supports in shape of buttresses rising up to rim of bowl.
Moulded rim.
Four angels in varying attitudes on underside of bowl at bottom of alternate angles.
Just below rim of bowl is a band of quatrefoils.
Between faces leaf carving runs down angle and across to opposite bottom corner.
Base octagonal with foliates on alternate angles between supports.
Font surrounded by iron railings.
On of the best fonts in Essex.

Cover

Said to be early nineteenth century but looks much earlier.
Octagonal with rosettes and various leaf shapes – one on each face.
Buttresses at angles with crockets.
Battlement decoration surrounds the base with small round-lobed quatrefoils under.
The cover is topped by a foliate finial.

O.S. Ref. No. 574 281

ST. NICHOLAS CHIGNAL SMEALEY

Church Foundation: Early sixteenth century.

Monopod. Octagonal bowl of brick. Early sixteenth century, Tudor.

Decoration

The font is quite undecorated except for moulding between pedestal and bowl. The bowl which is badly cracked is supported by an octagonal pedestal having alternatively four wide and four narrow sides.

The base is chamfered from base of pedestal and is octagonal.

This font is one of the few brick fonts in the country.

Cover

The cover is a flat raised octagonal lid with a floriated equal armed cross in wrought iron having a circle in the centre with fleur-de-lis in the spandrels. The handle is missing. Modern.

O.S. Ref. No. 668 116

ALL SAINTS & ST. FAITHS CHILDERDITCH

Church Foundation: Victorian, built on site of former church destroyed by fire.

Monopod. Octagonal bowl. Tudor, Sixteenth century.

Decoration

The small octagonal bowl is damaged and has a false rim. The faces are deeply recessed with square panels each of which has a pointed-lobed quatrefoil with a central foliate.

The underside of the bowl is moulded and has a hollow-chamfer and roll moulding to top of plain octagonal pedestal which has also been damaged. The bottom of the pedestal is finished with a roll moulding.

The small base is octagonal and hollow-chamfered to moulding and quirk on top of short vertical sides.

The whole is mounted on a square sub-base chamfered on the south-east and north-east corners.

Around the rim of the font is the following inscription: 'This is the cost of John Throsscher and Cecili his wife'.

Cover, Sixteenth century

The cover is composed of an octagonal flat wooden lid with moulded edge from which rises short sides pierced with stylised leaves. From inside rises a tall octagonal boarded concave cone with crocketed ribs rising to a large leaf finial which is not original but part of repair work.

O.S. Ref. No. 614 894

ST. PETER AND ST. PAUL — CHINGFORD

Church Foundation: Victorian, 1844.

Polypod. Square bowl, Purbeck marble. Transitional Norman, twelfth century.

Decoration

The bowl has five blank round-headed arches on each face. It was originally in All Saints the old church of Chingford and was transferred to St. Peter and St. Paul in 1844 when All Saints abandoned having fallen into a very bad state of disrepair. Fortunately the old church was restored in 1930 and is now used once again.

The central stem of the font is round with four round corner shafts with moulded bases mounted on a square base. The whole is mounted on a modern rectangular sub-base comprising a priest's step.

O.S. Ref. No. 389 944

ST. MARTIN OF TOURS — CHIPPING ONGAR

Church Foundation: Norman.

Monopod. Square bowl. Decorated, fourteenth century.

Decoration

Each face has two recessed trefoil-headed lancets.
Angles are chamfered with very large buttress-like supports rising to rim of bowl.
The bowl is mounted on an octagonal stem and base having hollow-chamfered top edge which are modern.
The whole is mounted on a square sub-base with priest's step.

Cover

The flat cover is octagonal and has four radiating trusses rising from alternate sides and meeting at the head of a central turned baluster shaped post just below the spike finial. Projecting from each truss is a carved foliate.

O.S. Ref. No. 554 029

HOLY TRINITY (Previously St. Mary) CHRISHALL

Church Foundation: Norman.

Polypod. Square bowl. Decorated, c1300 but could be earlier.

Decoration

The square bowl is plain and at some later date the top corner edges have been slightly chamfered. The base of the bowl is moulded.
The bowl is mounted on a drum central stem with four corner shafts. The north-east and south-west shafts are circular with square capitals, necking and roll moulding with square base surmounted with roll moulding. The south-east and north-west shafts are octagonal but otherwise similar to the other two shafts.

Cover

The cover is an octagonal lid surmounted with four convex curved panels each having a round-headed quatrefoil motif on each side. Where the panels meet in the centre of the lid there is a small Passion Cross. Modern.

O.S. Ref. No. 452 386

ST. MARY AND ST. CLEMENT — CLAVERING

Church Foundation: Perpendicular (built on site of earlier church)

Polypod. Octagonal bowl, Purbeck marble. Early English, thirteenth century.

Decoration

Each face contains two blank pointed arches. The stone of each arch opening has been left roughly cut.
The underside edge of bowl is chamfered.
The bowl is supported on a large octagonal central shaft with eight smaller supporting Purbeck marble shafts.
The whole is mounted on a massive modern octagonal base with added priest's step.

O.S. Ref. No. 471 318

HOLY TRINITY (now a museum) COLCHESTER

Church Foundation: Anglo-Saxon.

Monopod. Octagonal bowl. Perpendicular, fifteenth century.

Decoration

The octagonal bowl has large square recessed panels. The rim has been renewed.
When the church was converted into a museum the font was broken into pieces which have been skilfully put together.
East face: Pomegranite (?) and leaves.
North-east face: Uncharged shield surrounded by fruit and leaves.
North face: Leaves with central rose.
North-west face: Uncharged shield surrounded by fruit and leaves.
West face: Leaves with central rose.
South-west face: Uncharged shield surrounded by fruit and leaves.
South face: Leaves with central rose.
South-east face: Uncharged shield surrounded by fruit and leaves.
The shields contain graffiti.
The octagonal pedestal has a recessed trefoil-headed window form on each face and every alternate face has a buttress with set-off rising from the base.
The small octagonal base has a chamfered top edge and each alternate face has a square leaf on the chamfered edge. Under the chamfer is a deep quirk under which are short vertical sides.

O.S. Ref. No. 996 251

ST. MARY THE VIRGIN COPFORD

Church Foundation: Norman.

Polypod. Square bowl, Purbeck type. Transitional, circa 1200.

Decoration

Each face has four shallow blank round-headed arches.
The corner supports have unusual capitals which are decorated with what appear to be small round headed arches with a roll moulding and similarly in reverse at the bases. The central support also has three bands of roll moulding. The whole is raised on a modern stepped two slab base.

O.S. Ref. No. 935 226

ST. MARY-THE-VIRGIN CORRINGHAM

Church Foundation: Early Norman.

Polypod. Octagonal bowl. Early English, thirteenth century.

Decoration

The octagonal bowl has a chamfered rim edge and bottom edge. The faces are plain except for one which appears to have the remains of a carving in relief. The supporting shafts are made up of a large central shaft and four detached shafts. Two of the detached shafts are circular with square capitals having chamfered bottom edges finishing with a roll moulding. The other two shafts are square with chamfered outside edges and capitals similar to the circular shafts. The whole is mounted on a square base.

The font has been painted.

Cover

The cover is a flat wooden lid having a moulded edge. On top is an equal-armed iron cross having Fleur-de-lis ends and cable ring handle. Modern.

O.S. Ref. No. 709 834

ALL SAINTS CREEKSEA

Church Foundation: Originally Norman, rebuilt 1878 incorporating fragments of Norman church.

Monopod. Octagonal bowl. Perpendicular, fifteenth century.

Decoration

The octagonal bowl has a chamfered edge to the rim and the underside is also chamfered to the pedestal.
East face: Incised shield charged with a serpent all within an incised square.
North-east face: Incised saltire cross within an incised square.
North, north-west, west, south-west and south faces are plain.
South-east face: Incised saltire cross within an incised square.
The large octagonal pedestal is plain and the bottom is hollow-chamfered to the plain vertical octagonal base.

Old 'Font'

In addition to the Perpendicular font there is a rough unlined square stone bowl mounted on a modern square stone pedestal and base. This bowl measures twenty-four inches square and is thought to be dated c1125. It was found in the Creeksea glebe where it was used as a step to the barn. The bowl was replaced within the church in 1921.
Although this old bowl is thought to be the original font this is extremely doubtful owing to its size and that there is no drainage hole. It was probably a holy water stoup.

O.S. Ref. No. 931 969

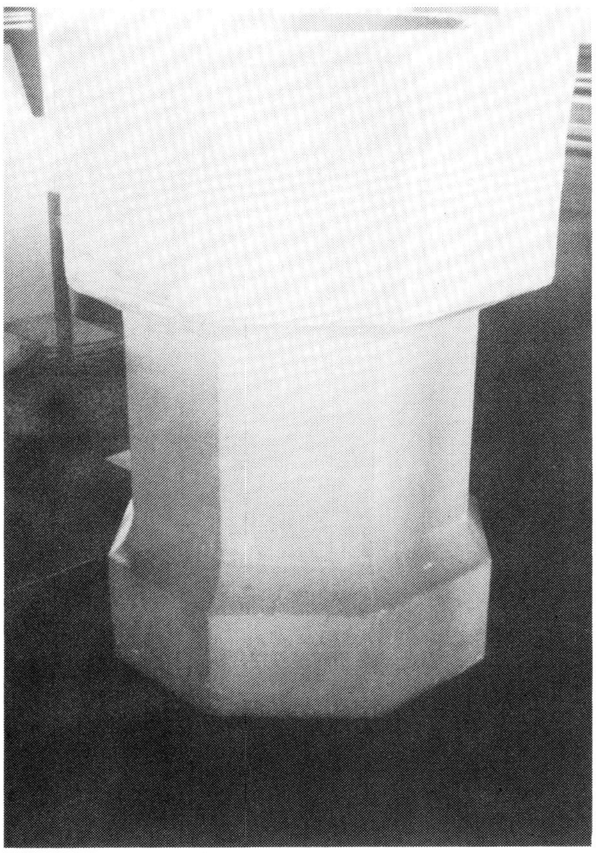

ST. MARY THE VIRGIN AND ALL SAINTS DEBDEN

Church Foundation: Early English.

Monopod. Octagonal bowl, Coade stone. Eighteenth century, Neo-perpendicular (1786).

Decoration

East face: Charged shield in round-lobed quatrefoil.
North-east face: Fleurette in round-lobed quatrefoil.
North-face: Star in round-lobed quatrefoil with name MUILMAN under.
North-west face: Fleurette in round-lobed quatrefoil.
West face: Arm with dagger in hand in round-lobed quatrefoil with name TRENCH under.
South-west face: Fleurette in round-lobed quatrefoil.
South face: Dove and olive branch in round-lobed quatrefoil with name CHISWELL under.
South-east face: Fleurette in round-lobed quatrefoil.
Octagonal pedestal: Each face carrying figures between corner buttresses.
East side: Charity.
North-east side: Hope.
North side: Justice.
North-west side: Prejudice.
West side: Life.
South-west side: Temperance.
South side: Fortitude.
South-east side: Faith.
This font was given by Mr. Richard Muilman Trench Chiswell in 1786. Coade stone is an artificial stone manufactured from c1769 at Lambeth, London, by Mrs. Eleanor Coade. Used for a variety of ornanmental purposes.

Cover

The octagonal cover is also made of Coade stone in the shape of an enclosed cone having concave ribs between the faces rising to a foliated finial. The sides of the base are decorated with five fleurettes to each side. The cover is hoisted by an iron chain counterpoised by a dove perched on a sphere.

O.S. Ref. No. 551 333

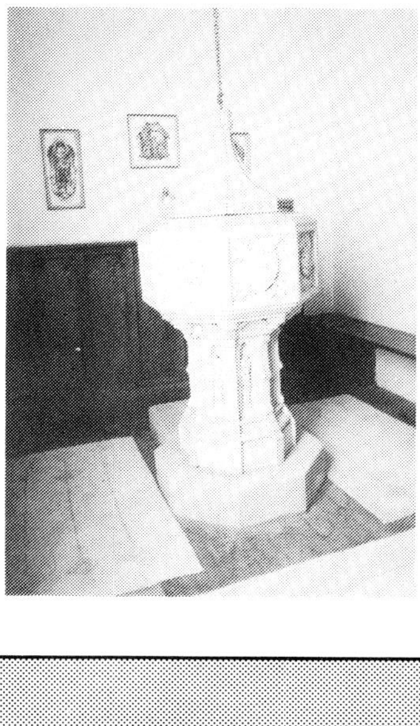

ST. MARY-THE-VIRGIN — DEDHAM

Church Foundation: Perpendicular (on site of either a Saxon or Norman church which was replaced by an early fourteenth century church).

Monopod. Octagonal bowl. Decorated, fourteenth century.

Decoration

The octagonal bowl is very mutilated. It is decorated with the emblems of the four Evangelists, the Lion, the Man, the Bull and the Eagle with angels in the alternate faces. The under edge of the bowl is decorated with a fringe of cherub heads with interlacing wings. The figures are, unfortunately, very defaced. The later octagonal pedestal is short and the base appears to have belonged to one of the fourteenth century church piers.

The rim of the bowl has marks of lid fastenings.

Cover

The circular wooden cover is Victorian and was made in 1861 by a village carpenter named Barber from the oak timbers of the warship Royal George which sank off Portsmouth in 1782. It has a moulded lower edge and rises four inches to a flat boarded lid with equal-armed iron cross and circle with four fleur-de-lis decorations around the circle which are painted gold.

Round the top edge of the cover is carved in Greek lettering the palindromic anagram which translated reads ‘Cleanse the sin not the appearance only’. This anagram is in the church of Santa Sophia in Constantinople.

Round the side of the cover is a brass band engraved with the words, ‘Suffer the little children to come unto me’.

O.S. Ref. No. 059 332

ALL SAINTS DODDINGHURST

Church Foundation: Early English.

Monopod. Octagonal bowl. Decorated, late fourteenth century.

Decoration

The font has been whitewashed and requires a thorough cleaning.

The rim of the octagonal bowl has been much repaired and the faces contain square recessed panels.

East face: Round-lobed quatrefoil within a circle with a face amid four leaves in centre (Green Man).

North-east face: Round-lobed quatrefoil within a circle with a square floriate amid four leaves in centre.

North face: Round-lobed quatrefoil within a circle with a square floriate amid four leaves in centre.

North-west face: Round-lobed quatrefoil within a circle with a square floriate amid four leaves in centre.

West face: Round-lobed quatrefoil within a circle with three leaves from central stem in centre.

South-west face: Round-lobed quatrefoil within a circle with a square floriate amid four leaves in centre.

South face: Round-lobed quatrefoil within a circle with a square floriate amid four leaves in centre.

South-east face: Round-lobed quatrefoil within a circle with a square floriate amid four leaves in centre.

The bowl is lipped at the top and bottom edges and is hollow-chamfered on the underside to a half-round moulding at the top of the pedestal.

The large pedestal is octagonal and each face has two cinquefoil headed window forms.

The octagonal base is moulded and hollow-chamfered to a deep quirk above short vertical sides. This is modern.

Cover

The cover is a circular boarded lid with an equal-armed iron cross having large Fleur-de-lis ends and a circular band in the centre of which is an iron loop-drop handle with round backplate. Modern.

O.S. Ref. No. 589 990

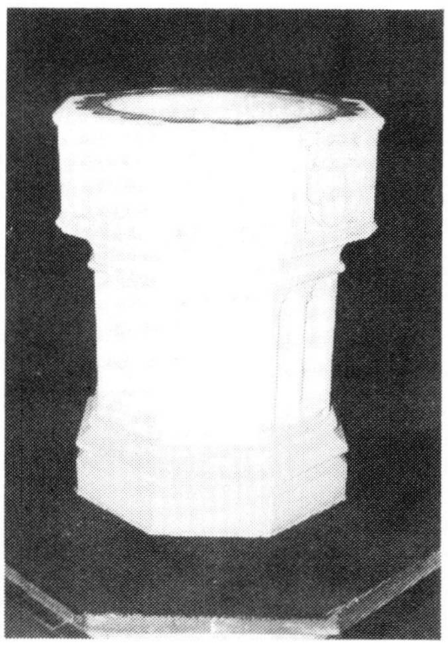

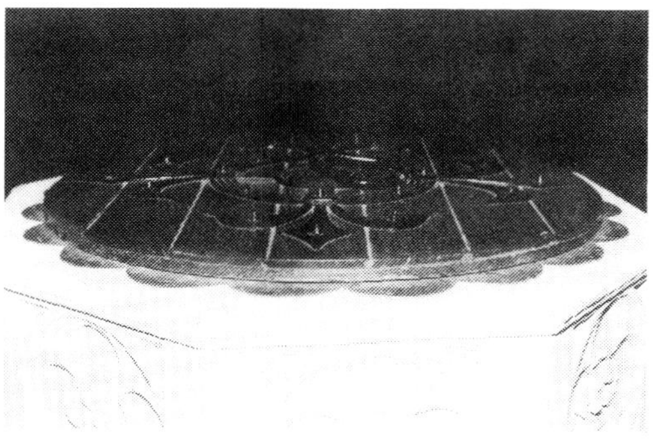

ALL SAINTS DOVERCOURT

Church Foundation: Norman.

Monopod. Octagonal bowl. Perpendicular, fifteenth century.

Decoration

The rim of the octagonal bowl has been damaged and repaired as indeed has other parts of the font.
The faces of the bowl are decorated in panels.
East face: Cusped equal armed cross (Greek) within a cusped lozenge.
North-east face: Four cinquefoil-traceried window forms with pointed quatrefoils over.
North face: Cusped lattice.
North-west face: Four cinquefoil-traceried window forms with pointed quatrefoils over.
West face: Four squared cusped quatrefoils in corners with a diagonal in centre having barbed ends.
South-west face: Four cinquefoil-traceried window forms with pointed quatrefoils over.
South face: Large cusped pointed quatrefoil with a cross in centre having barbed ends.
South-east face: Three cinquefoil-traceried window forms.
The square pedestal is moulded at top and bottom and the angles are worked into shafts. Between the shafts the sides are ridge moulded.
The square base has rounded angles and the whole is mounted on an octagonal modern sub-base.

Cover

The cover is composed of a flat octagonal wooden lid of oak boards.
Inset from the edge of the lid is a shallow square box the sides of which are pierced with pointed trefoils. There is a central cusped quatrefoil shaped baluster and four crocketed and cusped ribs rise from the angles to just below the top of the baluster. There are also cusped supports on the top of the box from the angles to the base of the baluster.
The triangle between the ribs, central baluster and supports resembles a large pointed unequal trefoil.
The baluster terminates in a foilate finial. Modern.

O.S. Ref. No. 238 312

ST. EDMUND KING AND MARTYR EAST MERSEA

Church Foundation: Perpendicular.

Monopod. Octagonal bowl. Perpendicular, fifteenth century.

Decoration

The bowl is large, deep and very beautifully decorated. Unfortunately it has been damaged in various places but must have been a very pretty font in its early years.

The rim edge is hollow chamfered with three fleurettes to each face.

East face: Crocketed cinquefoiled ogee arch with two trefoil headed window forms in each spandrel over. Small empty pedestal at base.

North-east face: Crocketed ogee arch with three-light traceried window form with two trefoil-headed window forms in each spandrel over. Small empty pedestal at base.

North, west and south faces: Similar to the east face.

North-west, south-west and south-east faces: Similar to the north-east face.

The bottom edge of the bowl is moulded and chamfered to stem each corner having a winged angel.

The stem is octagonal with crocketed ogee cinquefoiled arch with empty pedestal at base on each face.

Octagonal base has hollow-chamfered top with quirk just below edge and straight sides.

Cover

The wooden cover is a pointed octagonal cone having enclosed concave ribs ending in baluster type finial.

The cone is painted with leaf and flower design in grey and white. The finial is gold, red, and grey and the bottom edge of the cover is black with red line.

O.S. Ref. No. 051 142

ST. CATHERINE — EAST TILBURY

Church Foundation: Norman (transitional).

Monopod. Octagonal bowl. Late perpendicular, sixteenth century.

Decoration

The octagonal bowl has plain faces but the underside is moulded and has a hollow-chamfer to pedestal.

The short pedestal has plain sides and half-round moulding between it and the base.

The top of the base is widely hollow-chamfered to shallow sides.

Cover

The cover is a flat wooden lid with carved studded edge. Wrought iron equal armed cross decorated with flowers and leaves and four armed cross handle. Modern.

O.S. Ref. No. 689 769

ST. LAURENCE AND ALL SAINTS EASTWOOD

Church Foundation: Norman (it is believed that there was a chapel on this site prior to the present church).

Unmounted, bucket-shaped. Circular bowl, straight sided. Norman, late twelfth century.

Decoration

The circular bowl is tapered with encircling intersected round-headed blank arcading with slender piers and rests on a low moulded plinth which looks later. The whole may well be Transitional as the moulding on the plinth is an approximation to what was to be the characteristic base of early Gothic architecture, the 'water holding hollow'.

The rim of the bowl is damaged where hasp and staple have been broken away but part of the staple remains in situ. The bowl has been repaired in places. The whole is mounted on a modern circular base with priest's step.

O.S. Ref. No. 862 888

ST. MARY ELSENHAM

Church Foundation, Norman.

Monopod. Small round bowl. Eighteenth century.

Decoration

Small round bowl having fluting around lower half.
The bowl is mounted on an octagonal Gothic Revival pedestal each of which has a deeply recessed trefoil-headed lancet with mouldings at top and base.

Cover

Round wooden cone-shaped boarded cover rising to a baluster finial. Modern.

O.S. Ref. No. 543 259

Church Foundation. Early English.

Square rim to round bowl. Early English, thirteenth century.

Decoration

The small bowl, nineteen and a half inches square, has a square rim and is roughly finished showing chisel marks and a large blemish, by way of a depression, in the stone. This bowl is supported on an iron stand and is said to be the original font c1300.

It is felt, however, that it is not a font but a holy water stoup which would have been let into the wall near the entrance door where only the rim and inside of the bowl would have been seen. There are no marks of lid fastenings on the rim, the bowl has no drainage hole and there is no evidence that there have ever been any supports attached to it. The bowl is badly cracked which could have been caused when it was taken out of the wall during 'restoration'.

Cover, Jacobean

The present font at the west end of the church is Victorian but it has a cone-shaped wooden cover composed of an octagonal lid moulded on its edges and having straight ribs rising from the angles to the finial which is in the shape of a 'pupee' head. Each rib is decorated with a shallow leaf design running the length of the rib which has four crockets.

The cover is suspended by a cord over two small pulleys and is counter-balanced by a round iron weight.

O.S. Ref. No. 444 046

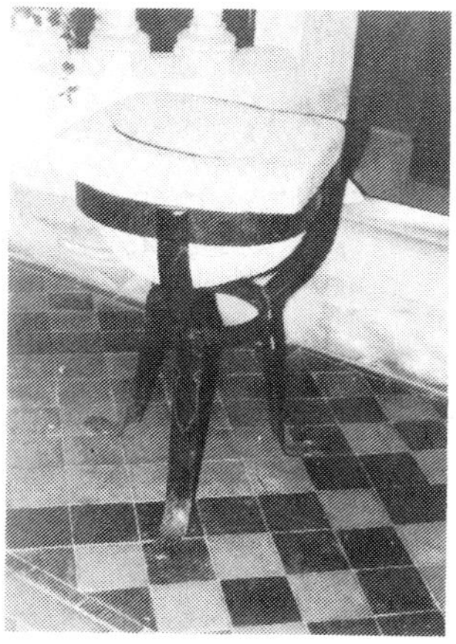

ST. GERMANS FAULKBORNE

Church Foundation. Norman.

Monopod. Octagonal bowl. Perpendicular, c1450.

Decoration

The octagonal bowl is unusual and similar to the Prittlewell and Ashingdon fonts in having concave faces which, in this case are plain.
The rim contains remains of lid fastenings.
The underside of the bowl is double hollow-chamfered to a half-round moulding at top of plain octagonal pedestal. The pedestal has half-round moulding at the bottom and the top of the octagonal base is hollow-chamfered with a deep hollow under to straight shallow sides.
The whole is mounted on a large octagonal sub-base.

Cover

The octagonal flat wooden cover has a moulded edge with a delightful wrought-iron equal armed cross having foliated ends together with other foliations and cable ring handle. Modern.

O.S. Ref. No. 800 166

HOLY CROSS FELSTED

Church Foundation. Norman.

Polypod, pedestal and shafts modern. Square top with circular bowl. Norman, late twelfth century.

Decoration

Human heads at corners connecting the circular bowl with square upper part.
Font very worn.
It is said that the bowl was found in the bed of the River Chelmer and was probably ejected from the church by the Puritans.
Shafts, pedestal and base are modern.

O.S. Ref. No. 678 204

ST. JOHN — FINCHINGFIELD

Church Foundation: Norman.

Monopod. Octagonal bowl. Decorated, fourteenth century c1375.

Decoration

The edge of the rim of the bowl is chamfered and each face has a shield with a carved device superimposed on a deeply recessed round-lobed quatrefoil within a circle.
The underside of the bowl has foliates and projecting corbelled heads of angels with outspread wings.
The short octagonal pedestal has a high moulded base. Modern.
The shields are charged.
East face: Lion rampant (Colvile)
North-east face: Chevron.
North face: Chevron with a small cross in each top corner and one under the chevron (Wycliffe).
North-west face: Diagonal barbed cross.
West face: Double chevron each having vertical arrows on each arm.
South-west face: Five pointed star or mullet in first quarter, plain raised field in second and third quarters with blank field (de Vere).
South face: Fret (de Mandeville).
South-east face: Cross.

O.S. Ref. No. 686 328

ST. ANDREW (Probably originally St. Ouen) FINGRINGHOE

Church Foundation: Norman.

Monopod. Octagonal bowl. Perpendicular, fifteenth century.

Decoration

The octagonal bowl has plain faces and a moulded underside to pedestal.
The octagonal pedestal is also plain.
The octagonal base has a deep moulded chamfered top.

Cover

The octagonal cover is probably sixteenth century and has been much repaired.
It rises in three stages to approximately eight feet.
The first stage has pierced buttresses with pinnacles at the angles. Between each buttress there are three plain panels topped with traceried heads. The panels are divided horizontally by strips with scalloped motif.
Two of the sides are hinged to form doors to open for baptism.
The second stage is a smaller octagon with pierced buttresses, plain panelling with scalloped motif strips and embattled top.
The top stage has openwork crocketed ogee ribs ending in a five leaved finial.
The inside of the case has blind tracery in the roof with a single drop pendant.
The cover is fixed to the rim of the font.

O.S. Ref. No. 029 204

ST. MICHAEL — FOBBING

Church Foundation: Anglo-Saxon.

Polypod. Octagonal bowl, Purbeck marble. Early English, thirteenth century.

Decoration

The octagonal bowl has two shallow blank trefoiled pointed arches on each face. The bowl is damaged where the lid fastenings have been removed. It rests on a round central pedestal and eight slender plain round supporting shafts mounted on a stepped octagonal base the two top edges being hollow-chamfered. The whole is mounted on a rectangular sub-base with chamfered top edge and corners on eastern side. All this is modern.

Cover

The cover is composed of an octagonal lid on which is mounted a shallow enclosed octagonal-sided drum. From the drum rises four ogee trusses attached to a tall turned baluster central shaft. Modern.

O.S. Ref. No. 718 839

Church Foundation: Norman.

Polypod. Square bowl, Caen stone. (Base, pedestal and supports modern). Norman, c1200.

Decoration

North face: Vine leaves.
West face: Cross and Crown.
South face: Sun, Moon and Stars.
East face: Tree of Jesse.
The rim has hasp and staple marks.

Note

The Norman fonts at Abbess Roding and Little Laver are similar so far as the trails of foliage or vine are concerned. These two churches and Fryerning are known to have been connected with relations or friends of Matilda, mother of Henry II and it may be that Matilda donated these three fonts.

O.S. Ref. No. 638 002

ST. NICHOLAS FYFIELD

Church Foundation: Norman.

Monopod. Square bowl, Purbeck marble. Transitional, late twelfth century.

Decoration

East and north faces: Each face has a leaf at each side with a fleur-de-lis or trefoiled foilage in centre.

South and west faces: Each face has a row of six shallow blank round-headed arches.

Hasp marks on rim.

Plain octagonal pedestal mounted on square base which is much later, probably fourteenth century.

The font is situate at the west end of the thirteenth century north aisle and has obviously been moved from its original position.

O.S. Ref. No. 572 068

ST. MARY-THE-VIRGIN GESTINGTHORPE

Church Foundation: Early English, (possibly on site of pre-conquest church).

Monopod. Octagonal bowl. Perpendicular, late fourteenth century.

Decoration

East face: Evangelist symbol for St. Mark (Winged Lion).
North-east face: Uncharged shield within an octfoil.
North face: Evangelist symbol for St. Luke (Winged Bull).
North-west face: Uncharged shield within an octfoil.
West face: Blank.
South-west face: Rosette within round-lobed quatrefoil.
South face: Evangelist symbol for St. John (Eagle).
South-east face: Rosette within an octfoil.
Underside of bowl is moulded to stem.
It is unusual to find only three of the Evangelists' symbols. St. Matthew's is missing.
The stem is octagonal and damaged.
The faces of the stem have various traceried window forms except the west face which is blank.
The base is chamfered with fleurettes on each face and a deeply cut quirk under.
The blank faces on the west side leads one to suppose that at some time the font stood against a wall or pier.

Cover

The octagonal wooden cover is flat with a wrought iron crown in the centre surmounted by a four-armed cross. Modern.

O.S. Ref. No. 812 386

ST. PETER AND ST. PAUL — GRAYS

Church Foundation: Norman.

Monopod. Octagonal bowl. Perpendicular, fifteenth century.

Decoration

The bowl has a moulded rim which is damaged.
Each face has deeply recessed panels.
East face: Round-lobed quatrefoil containing a fleurette.
North-east face: Round-lobed quatrefoil containing an uncharged shield.
North face: Round-lobed quatrefoil containing four petal floriate.
North-west face: Round-lobed quatrefoil containing a charged shield.
West face: Round-lobed quatrefoil containing floriate.
South-west face: Round-lobed quatrefoil containing uncharged shield with graffiti cross.
South Face: Round-lobed quatrefoil containing the Lamb, a Serpent and Rays of Glory symbolising Christ in Glory overcoming Evil through the Sacrament of Baptism.
South-east face: Round-lobed quatrefoil containing uncharged shield and graffiti.
The underside of the bowl is heavily moulded with hollow-chamfer to half-round moulding at top of pedestal.
The octagonal pedestal has deeply recessed panels on each face each of which contains a plain pointed arch.
The base is double hollow-chamfered.
Both pedestal and base are damaged.
The whole is mounted on a half-octagon sub-base.

Cover

The cover is a shallow pyramidal wooden lid with moulded edge, ribbed at angles and boarded. Between each of the ribs is carved a trefoil in relief.
In the centre of the cover is the tall figure of Christ with one arm raised in blessing and the other holding an infant child. A very nice piece of modern carving.

O.S. Ref. No. 613 777

ST. MARY-THE-VIRGIN GREAT BENTLEY

Church Foundation: Norman.

Monopod. Octagonal bowl. Perpendicular, late fourteenth century.

Decoration

The octagonal bowl is very damaged especially round the rim which has the remains of a moulded edge.
The font stands on the north side of the nave and has been moved from its original position on the south side which was the principal entrance. East, north, west and south faces each have a large uncharged shield within a panel. North-east, north-west, south-west and south-east faces each have two trefoil-headed window forms.
The underside of the bowl has a two-stepped chamfer with moulding between. On each face of top chamfer are two square floriates.
The octagonal pedestal has a plain lancet window form on each face.
The base is octagonal and has a half-round moulding with stepped chamfers and moulding to vertical sides.

Cover

The cover is a flat octagonal polished wooden lid with an equal armed cross having fish-tail ends and a central cable ring handle. Modern.

O.S. Ref. No. 109 217

ST. MARY MAGDALENE GREAT BURSTEAD

Church Foundation: Norman (on site of wooden Saxon church c680).

Monopod. Octagonal bowl. Perpendicular, early fifteenth century.

Decoration

The octagonal bowl is plain the underside being hollow-chamfered to a half-round moulding at the top of a plain octagonal pedestal which also has a half-round moulding at the bottom.
The octagonal base has a hollow-chamfered top to shallow vertical sides.
There are marks of lid fastenings on the rim.
The whole is mounted on a large octagonal sub-base.
The font shows damage in all parts.

Cover

The cover is formed by a concave copper lid engraved with three Latin crosses with rays of glory. Fixed to the cover are two small holders for candles. Modern.

O.S. Ref. No. 681 923

ST. JOHN THE BAPTIST — GREAT CLACTON

Church Foundation: Norman.

Monopod. Octagonal bowl. Perpendicular, fifteenth century.

Decoration

The octagonal bowl must have been very beautiful in its early days but regretfully, it is now much defaced. The rim has been damaged where the lid fastenings have been removed but has been repaired.

The panelled faces are deeply recessed and carved with three seated figures and winged angels, two holding charged shields. The panels are divided by niched buttresses.

East face: Seated figure.
North-east face: Seated figure.
North face: Winged angel.
North-west face: Winged angel holding a charged shield.
West face: Winged angel.
South-west face: Winged angel holding a charged shield.
South face: Winged angel.
South-east face: Seated figure.

The underside of the bowl is hollow-chamfered to a broken string-course moulding at the top of the short octagonal pedestal which has an octagonal base with moulded top.

The whole is mounted on a modern rectangular sub-base with two chamfered corners and comprising a priest's step.

Cover

The cover is a flat wooden lid with a wooden Latin cross. Modern 1954.

O.S. Ref. No. 176 165.

ST. PETER-AD-VINCULA GREAT COGGESHALL

Church Foundation, Perpendicular.

Polypod. Circular bowl. Early English, thirteenth century.

Decoration

Decoration on the bowl consists of shallow trefoiled head lancets. The bowl is mounted on a central column with roll moulding at the base and four supports having roll moulding, bell and necking at top and roll moulding at the bottom. The whole rests on a circular stone base.

The supports and base look much later but in keeping with the Early English style.

O.S. Ref. No. 859 231

ST. MARY   GREAT DUNMOW

Church Foundation: Decorated.

Monopod. Octagonal bowl. Decorated, fourteenth century.

Decoration

Panelled faces.
East face: Uncharged shield within lozenge with long-lobed trefoil in each corner of face.
North-east face: Three traceried window forms of period.
North face: Fleurée cross within round-lobed quatrefoil.
North-west face: Two long-lobed cusped quatrefoils over four trefoiled-head lancets.
West face: Uncharged shield within cusped octfoil.
South-west face: Two dagger quatrefoils surmounting a long-lobed quatrefoil and four long-lobed trefoils.
South face: Uncharged shield in round-lobed quatrefoil within a circle.
South-east face: long-lobed quatrefoil.
Moulded rim to font bowl.
The underside of the bowl has foliate decoration on each face.
The octagonal pedestal contains four cinquefoiled-head lancets in two tiers on each face.
Octagonal base has top edge chamfered. The whole is mounted on a step.

Cover

The octagonal cover is a tall pointed cone boarded with slender ribs rising to a finial. The boarded sides each have three vari-sized stars, possibly symbolizing regeneration.
The lower part of the cover just above the chamfered lid is carved on each side with vine leaves and grapes.

Old Disused Font Bowl

This disused font bowl is on the floor to the north-west of the present font. It is square with chamfered corners having attached buttresses. It is badly damaged and unmounted.
It is not possible to decipher the face against the wall and another is unrecognisable. The third face has three traceried lancets and the fourth face has four pointed-lobed quatrefoils and four traceried lancets.

It would appear to be early fourteenth century but why the church should have had two font bowls of the same period is not known.

O.S. Ref. No. 629 229

ALL SAINTS GREAT HORKESLEY

Church Foundation: Norman.

Monopod. Octagonal small bowl. Modern.

Cover

Date unknown possibly sixteenth century originally.
The octagonal cover is in three stages. The highest stage is crocketed with floriated finial.
The middle stage is buttressed and crocketed over a boarded centre.
Lowest stage buttressed with pierced tracery sides with moulded base surmounted with scalloped pattern.
The cover has been much repaired and is now mostly nineteenth century.
Raised by counterpoise weight.

O.S. Ref. No. 324 971

ST. MARY — GREAT LEIGHS

Church Foundation: Norman.

Monopod. Octagonal bowl. Perpendicular, late fourteenth century.

Decoration

The octagonal bowl is chamfered on the rim which is damaged by removal of lid fastenings.
East face: Round-lobed quatrefoil with fleuron in centre.
North-east face: Round-lobed quatrefoil with fleuron in centre.
North face: Round-lobed quatrefoil with fleuron in centre.
North-west face: Round-lobed quatrefoil with fleuron in centre.
West face: Round-lobed quatrefoil wiht shield charged with diagonal cross in centre.
South-west face: Round-lobed quatrefoil with fleuron in centre.
South face: Round-lobed quatrefoil with charged shield. The device is not recognised.
South-east face: Round-lobed quatrefoil with fleuron in centre.
The pedestal is later than the bowl and is probably fifteenth century. It has a half-round moulding at the top and each face has cinquefoiled tracery headed window form which is divided from the bottom of the pedestal by a form of transom. At the bottom are deeply recessed panels containing alternately round and pointed-lobed quatrefoils. The pedestal is much damaged on the east side. The floor of the church was raised during the reign of George III when it was paved with locally made large red tiles. This raising of the floor brought it level with the top of the base which is just visible.

Cover

The cover is a flat octagonal lid moulded on its edge with heavy raised acanthus leaves to each angle. In the centre is a raised foliate with berry finial. Modern.

O.S. Ref. No. 738 156

ST. GILES GREAT MAPLESTEAD

Church Foundation: Norman.

Monopod. Octagonal bowl. Perpendicular, c1400.

Decoration

This is an unusually tall and slender font with small bowl.
The rim has projecting moulding and each of the faces is carved with a round-lobed quatrefoiled circle enclosing a shield.
The font had been plastered and painted, probably in the seventeenth century, but in 1930 the plaster and paint which had disfigured it for so long was removed. Traces of the paint may still be seen but the removal revealed that the shields once bore painted Emblems of the Passion and had a border of green and yellow and red and yellow alternately. The Emblems which it is believed were painted on the shields during the last century were:

1. The Cross of Calvary.
2. The Reed, Sponge, Spear and Vinegar vessel on a pole.
3. The scourging Pillar and Rope.
4. The Lantern.
5. Intertwined Scourges with weighted ends.
6. The Seamless Coat and Dice.
7. The Crown of Thorns and Nails.
8. St. Peter's Cock which crowed thrice.

The underside of the bowl is moulded to the top of the pedestal where there is a band of alternate leaf and rosette carving.
Each face of the octagonal stem has deeply recessed tracery consisting of a trefoiled head lancet window form and originally were painted bright blue with thin yellow diapering which is still traceable.
The base is divided into two parts, the upper part being chamfered with projecting moulding and the lower part has the top edge hollow-chamfered. The whole stands on an octagonal sub-base with chamfered top edge. Modern.
The font used to stand beneath the tower arch but was removed to its present and original position during the restoration of 1861 when it was given a new sub-base.

O.S. Ref. No. 345 808

ALL SAINTS GREAT OAKLEY

Church Foundation: Norman.

Polypod. Square bowl, Purbeck marble. Norman, twelfth century.

Decoration

The square Purbeck marble bowl has blind arcading composed of five round-headed arches to each side the lower edge of the bowl being slightly moulded. The rim of the bowl has been damaged and repaired in places.
The bowl is supported on five independent shafts which are of very late twelfth century design and not contemporary with the bowl. They appear to be replacement shafts.
The base is square and would appear to be part of the original Norman font.

Cover, probably eighteenth century

The cover is a square lid made of oak planks with shallow vertical edging. It has a long wooden bar handle with a central support having a circular base decorated with concentric circles. The handle also had end supports.

O.S. Ref. No. 188 274

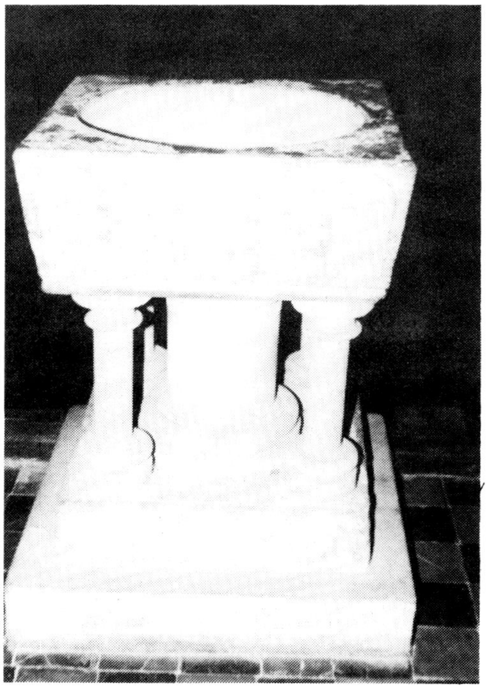

ST. MARY — GREAT PARNDON

Church Foundation: Perpendicular.

Monopod. Octagonal bowl. Perpendicular, fifteenth century.

Decoration

The octagonal bowl is small and has been damaged and repaired in places. There are marks where the lid fastenings have been removed together with graffiti.
The edge of the rim is chamfered.
East face: Recessed pointed-lobed quatrefoil with a floriate boss.
North-east face: Recessed pointed-lobed quatrefoil with a floriate boss.
North face: Recessed pointed-lobed quatrefoil with a shield charged with a bend (dexter to sinister).
North-west face: Recessed pointed-lobed quatrefoil with a floriate boss.
West face: Recessed pointed-lobed quatrefoil with a shield charged with a floriate.
South-west face: Recessed pointed-lobed quatrefoil with a floriate boss.
South face: Recessed pointed-lobed quatrefoil with a floriate boss.
South-east face: Recessed pointed-lobed quatrefoil with floriate boss.
The underside of the bowl is moulded and hollow-chamfered to half-round moulding at top of pedestal. Each face of chamfer has a floriate.
The octagonal pedestal is tall and decorated on all faces. The east, north-east, south-east, south and north faces each have a recessed window form of four lights each with a trefoiled head, two lights over and two under divided by a transom. The head of the window form contains a quatrefoil of three round-lobes and one pointed. The north-west, west and south-west faces each have a recessed window form of two lights, one above the other divided by a transom and each having a cinquefoiled head.
The octagonal base has a half-round moulding, chamfer and quirk to straight sides.
A priest's step has been added.

Cover

The wooden cover has a heavy wooden carving of Christ with children. It is dedicated 'To the Glory of God' in commemoration of the Coronation of King George V. 1911. Suffer little children to come unto me'. It was carved by Bertram Bishop headmaster of the church school.

O.S. Ref. No. 433 089

ST. JAMES THE GREAT — GREAT SALING

Church Foundation: Perpendicular.

Monopod. Octagonal bowl. Perpendicular, early fifteenth century (1410).

Decoration

East face: Two small round-lobed quatrefoils in circles above two trefoil-headed window forms.
North-east face: Two trefoil-headed window forms above four small trefoil-headed window forms.
North face: Uncharged shield within round-lobed quatrefoil within a circle.
North-west face: Two trefoil-headed window forms.
West face: Uncharged shield within lobes either side.
South-west face: Long-lobed pointed quatrefoil.
South face: Round-lobed quatrefoil within a circle.
South-east face: Four long-lobed pointed quatrefoils. Two over two.
The rim of the bowl is chamfered and has been damaged but repaired. The damage would appear to have been caused by removal of lid fastenings.
The base of the bowl is lipped with deep hollow-chamfer under to moulding and further hollow-chamfer to top of pedestal.
The short octagonal pedestal has an octagonal base with chamfered top edge.
The whole is mounted on a large octagonal sub-base with small priest's step. Modern.

O.S. Ref. No. 700 258

ST. MICHAEL GREAT SAMPFORD

Church Foundation: Early English.

Monopod. Octagonal bowl. Decorated, fourteenth century.

Decoration

The faces of the octagonal bowl are entirely plain. It is badly damaged around the rim some of the damage being caused by the removal of the lid fastenings. The under side of the bowl is moulded to the pedestal.
It is possible that the bowl is later than the pedestal.
The pedestal is short and each face has deeply recessed window tracery forms which vary with each face, under ogee arches. The bottom of the pedestal is moulded and mounted on a square base having spurs on the corners two of which have been badly damaged. The east and north sides of the base have been repaired with odd stonework.
The whole is mounted on a square sub-base with chamfered corners with priest's step. The sub-base has been repaired in brick on the east side.

Cover

The wooden seven-sided cover does not fit the font and was obviously made for a font which was built against a wall as it has four equal sides, two short sides and one long side. It is a concave ribbed and boarded pyramid rising to an octagonal pyramid finial.

O.S. Ref. No. 642 353

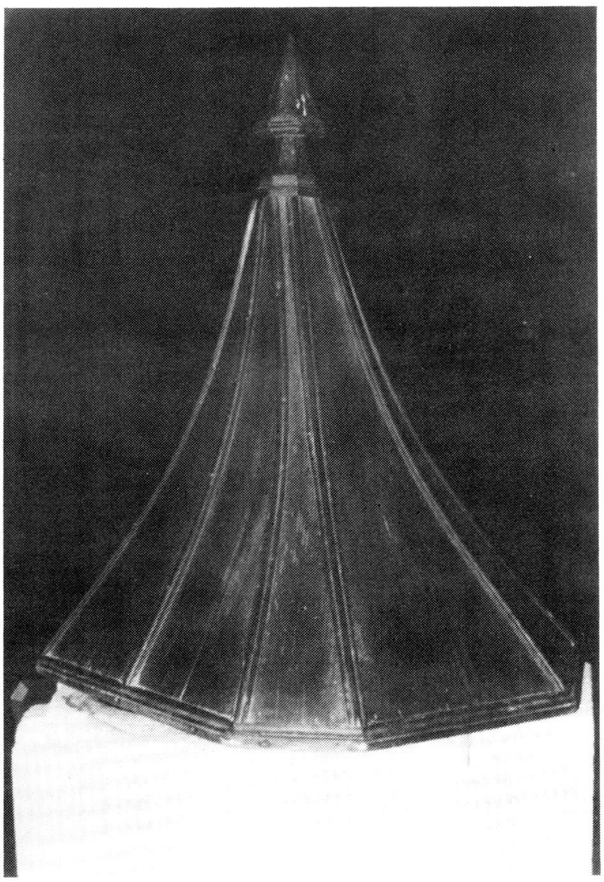

ST. MARY AND ALL SAINTS GREAT STAMBRIDGE

Church Foundation: Saxon.

Monopod. Octagonal bowl, Purbeck marble. Perpendicular, fifteenth century.

Decoration

The octagonal bowl has concave sides and shows marks of lid fastenings. The underside of the bowl on the north-west and west sides is badly damaged.

The faces are recessed and the underside of the bowl is moulded and hollow-chamfered to roll moulding at top of pedestal.

East face: Blank.

North-east face: Round-lobed quatrefoil in circle containing a shield charged with three four-pointed stars.

North face: Round-lobed quatrefoil in circle containing a shield charged with five horizontal bars.

North-west face: Round-lobed quatrefoil in circle containing a shield charged with an eight petalled flower.

West face: Round-lobed quatrefoil in circle containing a shield charged with a crown.

South-west face: Round-lobed quatrefoil in circle containing a crown charged with a four petalled rose.

South face: Round-lobed quatrefoil in circle containing a shield charged with a fleur-de-lis.

South-east face: Round-lobed quatrefoil in circle containing a shield charged with a four petalled rose.

The short octagonal pedestal and base have plain concave sides the top edge of the base being hollow-chamfered.

The octagonal stepped sub-base has a priest's step.

The bowl, pedestal and base are three separate parts which have been joined together comparitively recently judging by the cement used. Whether they were originally all together is not known.

Cover

The cover is a flat circular lid with wrought iron cross having arms ending in fleur-de-lis and triangular handle.

O.S. Ref. No. 895 907

ST. BARNABAS GREAT TEY

Church Foundation: Norman.

Monopod. Octagonal bowl. Perpendicular, fifteenth century.

Decoration

The rim of the bowl is moulded.

The faces have deeply recessed panels containing:

East face: Round-lobed quatrefoil within a circle and containing an uncharged shield.

North-east face: Round-lobed octfoil within a circle and containing an uncharged shield.

North face: Octfoil with pointed-lobed corner foils the remainder round-lobed and containing uncharged shield.

North-west face: Round-lobed octfoil within a circle and containing an uncharged shield.

West face: Octfoil with pointed-lobed corner foils the remainder round-lobed and containing uncharged shield which has graffiti.

South-west face: Round-lobed octfoil with uncharged shield.

South face: Round-lobed octfoil with uncharged shield.

South-east face: Round-lobed octfoil containing uncharged shield.

The underside of the bowl is moulded with fleurons on each face and has mutilated heads at the corners.

The pedestal is octagonal and each face has recessed window forms of four lights each with cinquefoiled head two lights over two lights under divided by a transom. Each panel contains differing forms of tracery.

The bottom of the pedestal is moulded and not mounted on a base.

The whole of the font is damaged in various places and has been painted or lime-washed. In its early days it must have been very fine.

Cover

The shallow convex oak lid is octagonal and has a raised moulded edge with narrow moulded ribs from the angles to the centre finial. 1975.

O.S. Ref. No. 892 258

ST. NICHOLAS GREAT WAKERING

Church Foundation: Norman.

Polypod. Square bowl. Early English, thirteenth century c1200.

Decoration

This font was acquired from East Horndon church in about 1970. The original Norman font was destroyed in 1907 because it was badly damaged and replaced by a Victorian font which is now in the Lady Chapel.
The corners and underside of the bowl are damaged but repairs have been made in places.
East face: Botonée cross.
North face: Intersecting blank arcading.
West face: Botonée cross.
South face: Intersecting blank arcading.
The bowl is mounted on a circular stem with four corner shafts having scalloped cushion capitals and moulded bases. Although the shafts are in keeping with the periuod they are modern as also is the stem.
The whole is mounted on a square base.

Cover

The cover is a square flat wooden lid with cut-off corners and has a wrought iron fleurée cross with central twist ring handle. Modern.

O.S. Ref. No. 949 875

ST. MARY AND ST. LAWRENCE GREAT WALTHAM

Church Foundation: Norman.

Monopod. Octagonal bowl. Early English, thirteenth century.

Decoration

The octagonal bowl has slightly tapered plain faces and a chamfered rim edge. The rim is much damaged where the fastenings securing the lid have been removed. The underside of the bowl is hollow-chamfered to pedestal.
The plain pedestal is octagonal on a small octagonal base.
The whole is mounted on a large square sub-base with priest's step.

Cover

The cover is a flat octagonal lid with a wooden handle mounted on a wooden Greek cross. There is an iron strap on each side of the handle. Modern.
In the south porch is the old Purbeck marble Norman font bowl which would seem to have had a shallow blank arcade of six round-headed arches on each side. The bowl is badly damaged. On the rim are marks of lid fastenings. The bowl is now mounted on a square base with two corner shafts and a support on the opposite side. These are modern.
This font was discovered under the floor in 1961 when the nave and chancel were re-floored.

O.S. Ref. No. 695 135

ST. STEPHEN — GREAT WIGBOROUGH

Church Foundation: Decorated.

Polypod. Octagonal bowl. Perpendicular, late fourteenth century.

Decoration

The bowl is octagonal with moulded top and lower edges and chamfered to stem.
East face: Pointed quatrefoil enclosing uncharged shield.
North-east face: Five petalled rose with thorns between each petal (Mystic Rose).
North face: Pointed quatrefoil enclosing uncharged shield.
North-west face: Two feathers quilted joined by a scroll (Resurrection).
West face: Pointed quatrefoil enclosing uncharged shield.
South-east face: Five petalled rose with thorns between each petal.
South face: Pointed quatrefoil enclosing uncharged shield.
South-east face: Five petalled rose with thorns between each petal.
The stem is octagonal with buttresses at alternate corners each having two set-offs. Base of stem is hollow-chamfered with vertical edge. The whole is mounted on a cruciform step on a rectangular base.

Cover

The cover is of the tabernacle type and counterpoised. The base is octagonal and moulded. It rises in three tiers with tracery carving and pinnacled buttresses. Modern.

O.S. Ref. No. 981 145

ST. JAMES-THE-LESS HADLEIGH

Church Foundation: Norman.

Polypod, originally monopod. Octagonal bowl. Early English, thirteenth century.

Decoration

The octagonal bowl has been chamfered on the outer edge of the rim, probably in order to disguise damage. A photograph on page 218 of Fonts and Font covers by Francis Bond (1908) shows the original edge quite clearly.

The faces are plain but the underside of the bowl is circular in plan and is decorated with trefoil stiff-leaf carved diagonally and seeming to grow out of the moulding at the base of the bowl.

The bowl now rests on a circular pedestal and four small circular detached shafts having Early English style capitals and bases with a circular base having a chamfered top edge. The whole is mounted on a circular sub-base with priest's step.

The bowl bears a Greek palindrome inscription, reading the same either forwards or backwards. The translation reads: 'Cleanse the sin, not the appearance only' or 'Cleanse you sin, not your face only'. This inscription was probably added in the fifteenth century or later.

According to George Buckler's book 'Churches of Essex' (1856) it would seem that at that time the font appears to have had a pedestal (monopod) and 'appears to have been circular but "worked down" to an octagon: the chamfered base is nearly buried by the floor which has been considerably raised'. It would appear from Buckler's description in 1856 and Bond's photograph of 1908 that new supports to the bowl incorporating thirteenth century style shafts replaced the octagonal pedestal sometime between these two dates.

Cover

The cover is an octagonal flat wooden lid with wrought iron equal-armed cross form with a crown at the end of each arm. In the centre is a serrated circle with plain ring handle. Probably Victorian.

O.S. Ref. No. 810 871

ST. BOTOLPH HADSTOCK

Church Foundation: Anglo-Saxon.

Monopod. Square bowl, (chamfered corners). Norman.

Decoration

The square bowl would appear to have been re-cut with chamfered corners leaving a protruding edge to form a base at the bottom.
The faces are plain and the bowl is mounted on a round pedestal built up of shallow curved stones probably re-used. The base is square with chamfered top edge.
The bowl has been much repaired especially on the north side.

O.S. Ref. No. 559 448

ST. ANDREW HALSTEAD

Church Foundation: Decorated.

Decoration

Monopod. Octagonal bowl. Perpendicular, c1420.

Decoration

East face: Shield charged quarterly 1 and 4 with arms of Stafford and 2 and 3 Bouchier and contained within an octfoil.
North-east face: Circle containing a round-lobed quatrefoil having a rosette in centre.
North face: Shield charged with Bouchier arms within an octfoil.
North-west face: Circle containing a round-lobed quatrefoil having a rosette in centre.
West face: Shield charged with arms of Peyton contained within an octfoil.
South-west face: Circle containing a round-lobed quatrefoil having a rosette in centre.
South face: Shield charged with arms of Peyton contained within an octfoil.
South-east face: Circle containing a round-lobed quatrefoil having a rosette in centre.
Moulded bowl rim and underside moulded and chamfered to stem, each face of the chamfer containing a fleurette. The bowl has been remounted on the present nineteenth century stem.
The stem is octagonal and contains a different form of window tracery on each face.
Base of stem is stepped with two rows of hollow chamfers.
The whole is mounted on an octagonal sub-base with priest's step.

O.S. Ref. No. 815 306

ST. NICHOLAS HARWICH

Church Foundation: Regency on site of a Norman chapel.

Polypod. Octagonal bowl, Purbeck marble. Early English, Early thirteenth century.

Decoration

The bowl of the octagonal font is cracked and the rim is damaged where lid fastenings have been removed. There are traces of colouring on the bowl. Each face has two shallow blank pointed arches.

The bowl is supported on a central shaft and seven smaller shafts all having moulded capitals and bases and mounted on a shallow octagonal base. The shafts and base are modern.

This font, which probably came from the old Chapel, was found in the churchyard and reinstated in the church in 1876.

Cover

The cover is a flat oak lid with moulded edge on which is mounted a shallow ogee-shaped cone rising to a knot finial. Modern.

O.S. Ref. No. 261 327

ST. JOHN THE EVANGELIST

HAVERING-ATTE-BOWER

Church Foundation: Victorian, (built on site of earlier church).

Monopod. Octagonal bowl, Purbeck marble. Norman, twelfth century from earlier church.

Decoration

Each face has two shallow blank round headed arches.
The rim has holes showing were lid fastenings have been removed.
The pedestal and base are modern in the Early English style.

Cover

Octagonal having curved boarded ribs with crockets. Finial decorated with buttresses and gabled recessed blank lancet window forms. Counterpoised using metal ball. Modern.

O.S. Ref. No. 511 931

ST. ANDREW HELION BUMPSTEAD

Church Foundation: Early English.

Monopod. Octagonal bowl. Perpendicular, fifteenth century.

Decoration

East face: Round-lobed quatrefoil in circle.
North-east face: Long-lobed pointed quatrefoil.
North face: Round-lobed quatrefoil in circle.
North-west face: Long-lobed pointed quatrefoil.
West face: Round-lobed quatrefoil within a circle.
South-west face: Long-lobed pointed quatrefoil integrated with round-lobed quatrefoil making a mixed multifoil.
South face: Long-lobed pointed quatrefoil.
South-east face: Long-lobed pointed quatrefoil.
Bottom of bowl is moulded.
Pedestal is octagonal with trefoiled head lancet on each face.
Bottom of pedestal is chamfered as also is the top edge of base which is mounted on octagonal step with priest's stone.

O.S. Ref. No. 652 416

ST. MARY THE VIRGIN — HENHAM

Church Foundation: Early English.

Monopod. Octagonal bowl. Perpendicular, Fifteenth century.

Decoration

East face: Shield charged with fiery cross in round-lobed quatrefoil within a circle.
North-east face: Shield charged with crucifix and symbols of the Passion in round-lobed quatrefoil.
North face: Shield charged with unidentified arms.
North-west face: Shield charged with fiery cross in first quarter and two money bags (?) in second, third and fourth quarters.
West face: Shield charged with unidentified arms.
South-west face: Shield charged with unidentified arms.
South face: Shield charged with unidentified arms.
South-east face: Shield appears to be uncharged but may have been previously charged.
The bowl is moulded on the underside.
The pedestal and base are octagonal with a trefoiled lancet on each face deeply inset.
The base is moulded but badly damaged.
Where bowl meets the pedestal repairs have been effected by fitting an iron band.

Cover

Wooden octagonal pyramidal cover with pierced trefoils on each face terminating with a turned finial.

O.S. Ref. No. 544 285

ST. ANDREW HEYBRIDGE

Church Foundation, Norman.

Polypod. Square bowl, Marble. Victorian, 1897.

Decoration

This font has been included because it is believed to be a copy of the original Norman Purbeck marble font. Parts of the original font are incorporated in the western jamb of the easternmost window in the north wall of the nave.
The bowl is square with four shallow blank round-headed arches on each of two faces and a diagonal cross on each of the other two faces.
The bowl is supported on a central drum stem and four corner supports each having water holding mouldings at their bases and mounted on a square base with chamfered top edge. The whole is mounted on a rectangular stone step.

Cover

Flat wooden circular cover with flat wrought iron four-armed cross having fleur-de-lis ends. In the centre is a ring handle.

O.S. Ref. No. 855 082

ST. MARY THE VIRGIN — HIGH EASTER

Church Foundation: Norman.

Monopod. Octagonal bowl. Early perpendicular.

Decoration

East face: Lion (St. Mark).
North-east face: Angel holding shield.
North face: Ox (St. Luke).
North-west face: Angel holding shield.
West face: Winged man (St. Matthew).
South-west face: Angel holding shield.
South face: Eagle (St. John).
South-east face: Angel holding shield.
The decoration on each face is recessed and four of the faces contain symbols of the Evangelists.
Between the bowl and the pedestal there is moulding.
The top of the bowl is very worn and damaged where the lid fastenings have been wrenched out. The bowl has been broken and repaired.
The lead lining contains graffiti.
The pedestal is square with partly chamfered angles leaving spurs on a square base.
The whole is mounted on a sub-base three sides of which are chamfered the remaining sides forming a large priest's step. Modern.

O.S. Ref. No. 619 148

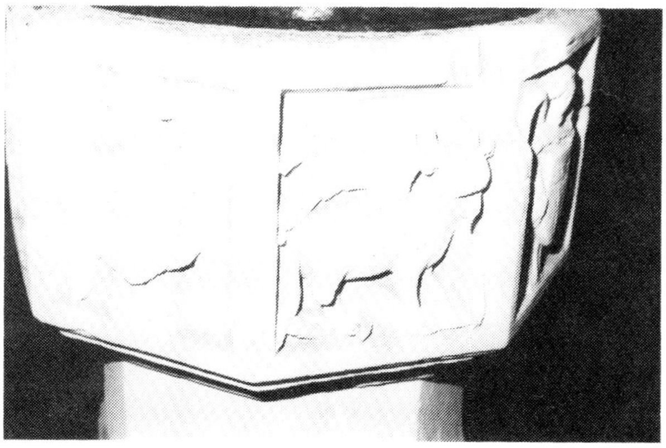

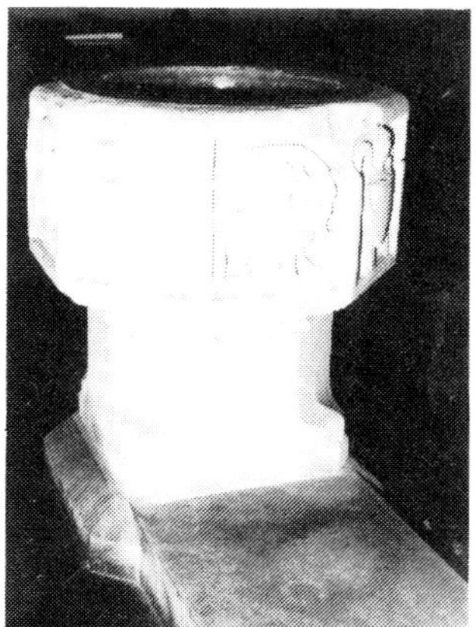

ALL SAINTS HIGH LAVER

Church Foundation: Norman.

Monopod. Octagonal bowl. Perpendicular, fifteenth century.

Decoration

Each face has a recessed round-lobed quatrefoil containing an uncharged shield.
The underside of the bowl is moulded and hollow-chamfered to stem.
The stem is octagonal each side containing two trefoiled lancet window forms with pointed head. Each head contains different form of tracery.
The base has had a long step inserted under part of the west side at a much later date leaving the base with five sides surmounted with double roll moulding.
There is graffiti on the bowl – 'TM 1719'.
This font is very similar to High Roding font.

O.S. Ref. No. 527 086.

ALL SAINTS — HIGH RODING

Church Foundation: Early English.

Monopod. Octagonal bowl. Perpendicular, early fifteenth century.

Decoration

Each face has a circle enclosing a round-lobed quatrefoil containing an uncharged shield.
The rim edge is chamfered and the underside of bowl is moulded and chamfered to half-round moulding at top of pedestal.
The pedestal is panelled with two lancets with head tracery. Lower part is nicely moulded.
This font is in fine condition which leads one to think that the carving has been preserved by being plastered over during the Commonwealth period or that it has been re-cut at some period.
This font is very similar to High Laver font.

O.S. Ref. No. 592 165

ST. PETER AND ST. PAUL — HOCKLEY

Church Foundation. Transitional, late twelfth century. (Possibly on site of earlier church).

Monopod. Octagonal bowl, Purbeck marble. Early English, c1180.

Decoration

The massive octagonal bowl of Purbeck marble is much damaged especially where the lid fastenings have been wrenched out. Part of a staple remains in situ.

Each face of the bowl contains two shallow pointed arches.

The bowl rests on an octagonal pedestal, which is now only part of the original, having the remains of shafts at the angles. It is now much shorter than the original and the base is missing.

The whole is now mounted on a deep modern octagonal base.

When the font was new it must have looked very delightful.

It is understood that the reason for its mutilated and weathered condition is that for many years it lay in fragments in the belfry, baptisms being performed in a wooden bowl set on a pedestal.

Cover

The wooden cover is very modern and ornate. It comprises an octagonal lid with moulded edge from which rise four convex trusses with centre baluster surmounted with a ball finial on which is a dove of peace. The cover is coloured blue, silver, gilt and white and was presented by Evelyn Mary Eileen Morgan 17/12/1967 and her husband Morgan Bronley Morgan, Priest, Vicar of Hockley 1935-67 d. 18/4/70.

O.S. Ref. No. 826 933.

ST. PETER AND ST. PAUL HORNDON-ON-THE-HILL

Church Foundation: Early English.

Monopod. Square bowl. Decorated, Fourteenth century.

Decoration

East face: Three square panels – centre panel blank – two end panels each has a long-lobed pointed quatrefoil.
North face: Similar to east face.
South face: Three square panels – centre panel blank – two end panels each has a cinque-foiled head lancet window form.
West face: Three square panels – centre panel blank – two end panels each has a round-lobed quatrefoil within a circle.
The pedestal is square.
East face: Double cinquefoiled head lancet window formation.
North face: Triple cinquefoiled head lancet window formation.
South face: Diagonal cusped cross.
West face: Cusped Greek cross within cusped circle.
The base is square with top edge chamfered.

Cover

The cover is octagonal cone shaped with straight ribs rising to a ball finial.

O.S. Ref. No. 669 836.

ST. NICHOLAS INGRAVE

Church Foundation: (Rebuilt in the eigheenth century on site of old church).

Monopod. Octagonal bowl. Perpendicular, fifteenth century.

Decoration

The rim of the octagonal bowl is chamfered on its lower edge and has been damaged by removal of lid fastenings but repaired.
Each face has two deeply recessed panels each containing a round-lobed quatrefoil.
The underside of the bowl is deeply hollow-chamfered to the pedestal terminating in a half-round moulding.
The octagonal pedestal is plain and roughly hewn.
The small base is octagonal and hollow-chamfered on the top edge to a quirk above shallow vertical sides.
The whole is mounted on a modern square sub-base.

O.S. Ref. No. 623 921

ST. NICHOLAS — KELVEDON HATCH

Church Foundation: Victorian (replacing earlier church near Kelvedon Hall).

Monopod. Octagonal bowl. Perpendicular, fifteenth century.

Decoration

The rim of the octagonal bowl is very worn.
The faces are recessed square panels.
East face: Small round-lobed quatrefoil within a circle in the centre of which is the head of a man.
North-east face: Small round-lobed quatrefoil within a circle in the centre of which is a fleuron.
North face: Small round-lobed quatrefoil within a circle in the centre of which is a bishop's mitre.
North-west face: Small round-lobed quatrefoil within a circle in the centre of which is a fleuron.
West face: Small round-lobed quatrefoil within a circle the centre of which is defaced.
South-west face: Small round-lobed quatrefoil within a circle in the centre of which is a fleuron.
South face: Small round-lobed quatrefoil within a circle in the centre of which is a fleuron.
South-east face: Small round-lobed quatrefoil within a circle in the centre of which is a crown.
The underside of the bowl is hollow-chamfered to a half-round moulding.
The octagonal pedestal has a deeply recessed cinquefoil headed window form on each face and has been considerably damaged.
The substantial octagonal base has a half-round moulding followed by a chamfer and further half-round moulding on top of low vertical sides. The lower part has vertical sides with chamfered top edge.
The whole is mounted on a large square two-stepped sub-base with priest's step. Modern.

Cover, Nineteenth century

The cover is an octagonal wooden lid with a tall octagonal wrought iron tendril ornamented cover. From the short vertical sides rises an octagonal cone the angle ribs having crockets. Above each of the vertical sides is a rosette. Very ornamental.
Above are crossed arms and a hook to a very ornamental chain which is attached via a pulley to a counterbalance weight.

O.S. Ref. No. 569 990

ST. NICHOLAS LAINDON

Church Foundation: Decorated.

Polypod. Square bowl, Purbeck type. Early English, thirteenth century.

Decoration

Each face has four blank pointed arches.
Round central stem with four round corner shafts mounted on square base.

O.S. Ref. No. 688 895

Church Foundation: Norman.

Monopod. Hexagonal bowl. Eighteenth century, Classical.

Decoration

Small hexagonal bowl of alabaster mounted as to part on a stone baluster stem with bulging lower part and as to part on top of square lower half. The whole mounted on a small square sub-base.

O.S. Ref. No. 478 961

ST. GILES LANGFORD

Church Foundation: Norman.

Monopod. Octagonal bowl. Perpendicular, fifteenth century.

Decoration

Each face is undecorated.
Underside of the bowl is chamfered to the pedestal where there is roll moulding.
The pedestal is octagonal and has roll moulding between it and the base.
The base is octagonal with a deep chamfered upper edge.
The whole is mounted on a circular sub-base with priest's step.

O.S. Ref. No. 838 090

ST. JOHN THE EVANGELIST — LANGLEY

Church Foundation: Norman.

Monopod. Octagonal bowl. Early perpendicular, circa 1400.

Description

The rough stone octagonal bowl has plain tapered faces. The rim and edge are damaged especially where the lid fastenings have been removed. The underside is stepped.

The octagonal pedestal looks to be of a later date than the bowl and is hollow-chamfered at the top with necking moulding. Probably modern.

The small base is chamfered on the top face.

The whole is mounted on a large shallow octagonal sub-base with priest's step.

Cover

The cover is a wooden octagonal lid with moulded edge and four radiating trusses from alternate sides and meeting at the centre on to a turned baluster-shaped post with ball finial. Probably Victorian but may be earlier.

O.S. Ref. No. 443 353

ST. MARY — LAWFORD

Church Foundation: Decorated.

Monopod. Round bowl. Classical, eighteenth century.

Decoration

The small plain round bowl has a moulded edge and resembles a basin.

The baluster stem is moulded where it joins the bowl and has an annulet a little lower down. Near the base the stem opens and is decorated with a form of gadroon moulding.

The shallow circular base has a moulded edge and is mounted on a modern small square stone block on a large rectangular sub-base having chamfered corners.

Covers

The cover is a round flat wooden lid with iron cable ring handle.

O.S. Ref. No. 089 316

Church Foundation: Norman.

Monopod. Octagonal bowl. Decorated, fourteenth century.

Decoration

The deep octagonal bowl has plain faces. The rim has been damaged but still retains two staples into which the cover was padlocked.

The underside of the bowl is moulded to the stem which is octagonal and plain.

The low octagonal base has a chamfered top edge.

Cover, Seventeenth century

The cover is a thin boarded octagonal lid with shaped serrated cross-piece as a handle with two further cross pieces (one either side) to serve as strengthening pieces. It has obviously been designed to fit the staples but it is doubtful whether it was ever secured.

The method of security would have been an iron bar through the tubular staples, supports and handle across the lid and padlocked. There are no holes in the supports or handle to allow the entry of a bar.

It may be that the original cross pieces and handle have been renewed or that when the cover was made it was never intended that it should be locked but merely to fit the existing staples.

O.S. Ref. No. 590 133

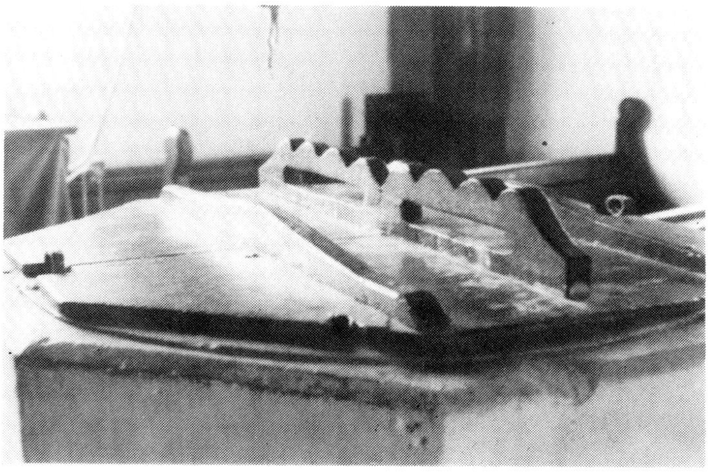

ST. MARY THE VIRGIN — LINDSELL

Church Foundation: Norman.

Monopod. Octagonal bowl. Perpendicular, fifteenth century.

Decoration

The bowl has a moulded rim and lower edge which are both damaged.
East face: Uncharged shield within a circle.
North-east face: Round-lobed quatrefoil within a circle.
North face: Uncharged shield within a circle.
North-west face: — Round-lobed quatrefoil within a circle.
West-face: Uncharged shield within a circle.
South-west face: Round-lobed quatrefoil within a circle.
South-face: Uncharged shield within a circle.
South-east face: Round-lobed quatrefoil within a circle.
On underside of bowl at each corner is a corbel of angled stone.
The pedestal is octagonal with niched buttress-like corners ending with chamfered edged base standing on an octagonal step.
Each face of the pedestal has three deeply cut panels containing:
Top: Round-lobed trefoil.
Centre: Round-lobed quatrefoil.
Bottom: Possibly a round-lobed trefoil but pedestal has been damaged making identification difficult.

Cover

Boarded octagonal cone with straight moulded ribs ending with a fleurée cross finial. Probably nineteenth century.

O.S. Ref. No. 644 271

DEDICATION UNKNOWN LISTON

Church Foundation: Norman.

Monopod. Octagonal bowl. Perpendicular, fifteenth century.

Decoration

The whole font is in a very poor state with much damage round the rim. The faces are believed to contain forms of round-lobed quatrefoils but it is difficult to distinguish. The underside is chamfered to the pedestal and composed of a band containing a fleurette on each face and a lower band of moulding.

The short pedestal has two recessed trefoiled head lancet window forms with transoms on each face and the base has roll moulding under which is a hollow-chamfer. The straight sides of the base have three round-lobed quatrefoils within circles to each face. The base is five-sided the remaining three sides being taken up with a priest's step.

O.S. Ref. No. 852 448

ST. MARY-THE-VIRGIN LITTLE BADDOW

Church Foundation: Norman.

The present font is a modern octagonal font which was placed in the church sometime in the 1950's.

Just to the east of the south door is a large circular trough which originally had four buttress-like grips round the bowl. These grips have been badly damaged and large pieces of them are missing. The base of the trough is flat. There is no drainage hole and it seems probable that it was a mortar used for melting lead to make leaden roofing sheets. The mortar is mounted on a mill-stone from a local water-mill. It is said that the trough was discovered in the nineteenth century in a garden in the adjoining parish of Boreham.

The date of the mortar is not known but may possibly be fifteenth or sixteenth century.

O.S. Ref. No. 764 081

ST. MARY THE VIRGIN — LITTLE BENTLEY

Church Foundation: Norman.

Monopod. Octagonal bowl. Perpendicular, c.1500.

Decoration

The rim of the octagonal bowl has been damaged and repaired with cement and an iron insert.

The faces of the bowl are plain with the exception of the east face which has a pointed-lobed octfoil with a central shield charged with a barbed chevron on which are three leopards heads, the arms of the Pyrton family.

The underside of the bowl is hollow-chamfered to a roll moulding at the top of the octagonal pedestal. The chamfer is decorated on the

East face: Fleurette.
North-east face: Uncharged shield.
North-face: Fleurette.
North-west face: Uncharged vertically ridged shield.
West face: Fleurette.
South-west face: Uncharged shield.
South face: Fleurette.
South-east face: Uncharged shield.
The octagonal base is moulded.

Cover

The cover is a flat octagonal wooden lid with an equal armed iron cross having fleur-de-lis ends and cable ring handle in centre. Modern.

O.S. Ref. No. 123 250

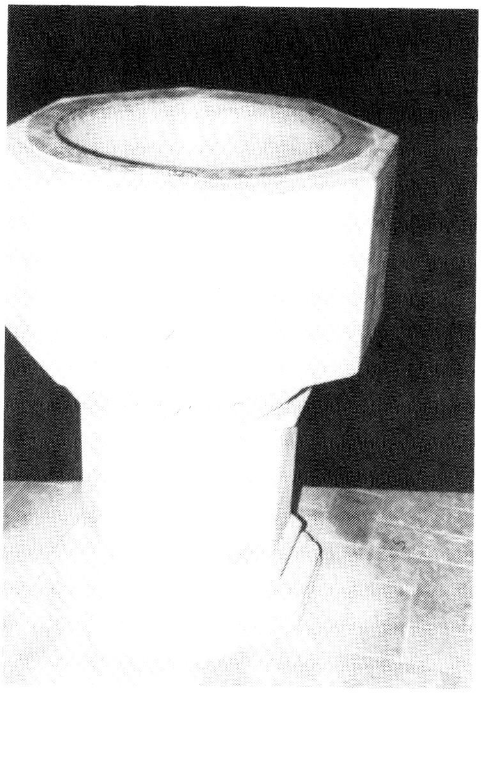

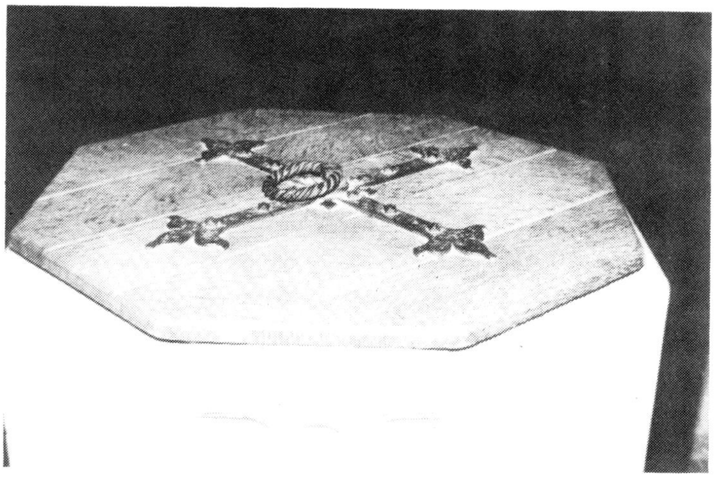

ST. MARY THE VIRGIN LITTLE BROMLEY

Church Foundation: Norman.

Monopod. Octagonal bowl. Purbeck marble. Perpendicular, fifteenth century.

Decoration

The rim of the octagonal bowl has been repaired and there are marks where the lid fastenings have been removed.
The faces are not orientated in line with the east-west axis of the church.
Four of the faces are rather crudely carved with the emblems of the Evangelists.
Approximately east face: Winged man — St. Matthew.
Approximately north face: Large rosette.
Approximately north face: Winged lion — St. Mark.
Approximately north-west face: Large rosette with leaves.
Approximately west face: Eagle — St. John.
Approximately south-west face: Large rosette.
Approximately south face: Winged ox — St. Luke.
Approximately south-east face: Large rosette.
At alternate angles on the underside of the bowl are winged angels.
The octagonal pedestal has buttresses, with one offset, at alternate angles coinciding with the winged angels.
The octagonal base has a chamfered top edge to vertical sides.

O.S. Ref. No. 092 277

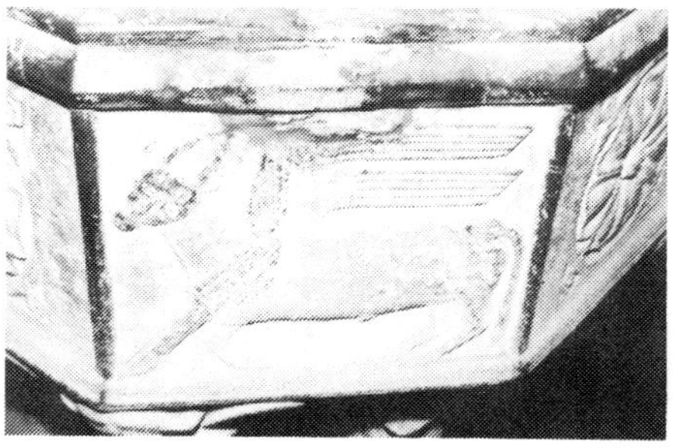

ST. MARY — LITTLE BURSTEAD

Church Foundation: Early English, (Possibly Norman)

Monopod. Octagonal bowl. Perpendicular, fifteenth century.

Decoration

The octagonal bowl is plain but has a heavily moulded underside chamfered to a half-round moulding. There is evidence of lid fastenings in rim.

The short octagonal pedestal is plain and separated from the base by a half-round moulding.

The octagonal base is chamfered to a deep quirk with shallow vertical sides under. The underside of the bowl, pedestal and base are damaged.

Cover

The cover is a flat stepped wooden lid having a wrought iron equal-armed cross with fleur-de-lis ends and cable ring handle. Modern.

O.S. Ref. No. 719 943

HOLY TRINITY LITTLEBURY

Church Foundation: Norman.

Polypod. Square bowl. Transitional Norman, twelfth century.

Decoration

Each face is plain.

The top of the pedestal has roll mouldings where it joins the bowl. The bottom of the pedestal is mounted on a small square base. The four corner shafts are octagonal with, square bases and capitals (cushion). Hidden by casing. The font is entirely encased in wood (oak) in the form of a case which is square and fixed to the floor. It is provided with double doors for access to the font similar to Thaxted and is square whereas Thaxted is octagonal.

The case is late fifteenth or early sixteenth century and is a marvellous piece of Tudor woodcarving. It is composed of three tiers of linen-fold panelling. The hinges are very fine being engraved with swords, hammers and other forms of decoration. The third tier has a carved cornice from which rises an elaborate pyramidal top with buttresses, niches, gables and pinnacles ending with a finial carved with a figure of St. John the Baptist.

O.S. Ref. No. 517 395

ST. MARY THE VIRGIN LITTLE CHESTERFORD

Church Foundation, Norman.

Monopod. Octagonal bowl, Early English, thirteenth century.

Decoration

The octagonal bowl has plain faces but the edge of the rim is chamfered, probably at a later date, and the underside is moulded.
There are marks of lid fastenings on some of the faces.
The pedestal is octagonal and plain.
The whole is mounted on a large octagonal sub-base.

O.S. Ref. No. 515 417

ST. JAMES — LITTLE CLACTON

Church Foundation: Norman.

Polypod. Square bowl, Purbeck type. Transitional, late twelfth century.

Decoration

All faces contain four blank shallow round-headed arches.
The central stem and four supports and base are modern.

Cover

The cover has a circular lid with moulded edge surmounted by a square stem with a finial similar to a double Greek cross (fleurée). From each side of the stem is a panel with moulded top edge ending with a moulded buttress having a trefoiled head lancet on each of the three faces.
Each panel has a pierced round-lobed quatrefoil. Modern.

O.S. Ref. No. 166 188

ST. MARY — LITTLE DUNMOW

Church Foundation: Early English (part of the Augustinian Little Dunmow Priory founded in 1106).

Monopod. Octagonal bowl. Decorated, fourteenth century.

Decoration

Undecorated faces which are shallow in depth. Underside of bowl is moulded and damaged.
Pedestal is octagonal with trefoiled-head lancet on each face.
The pedestal is mounted on octagonal base with chamfered top edge.
The whole is mounted on a modern base incorporating a priest's step.

Cover

The cover is wooden and octagonal with shallow concave boarded ribs terminating in moulded finial surmounted with a patée cross. Modern.

O.S. Ref. No. 655 213.

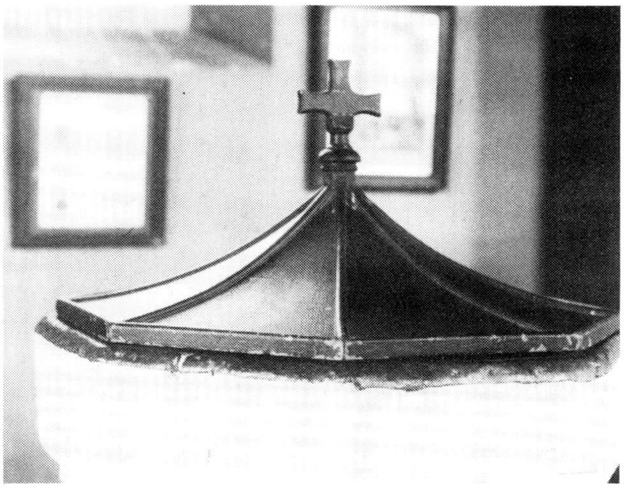

ST. MARY THE VIRGIN LITTLE LAVER

Church Foundation: Norman.

Polypod. Square bowl. Norman, c1200.

Decoration

East face: Fleurettes in each top corner with moon and sun in centre. Two large six petalled flowers on each side with whorl in centre.
North face: Two large round-lobed quatrefoils with fleurette in centre of each.
West face: Stylised leaf scroll.
South face: Three fleur-de-lis with a round disc between each and four round discs above.
It seems certain that the north and south faces have been re-cut.
The bowl is supported on a circular central pedestal and four plain circular detached corner shafts which are not original.
Small square base is plain.

Cover

The cover is octagonal, cone-shaped in three tiers with broaches on corners. Similar in design to a broach spire.
It is suspended by an iron chain over two small pulleys and counter-balanced by two decorative iron weights. Fifteenth century.

O.S. Ref. No. 544 097

ST. JOHN THE EVANGELIST — LITTLE LEIGHS

Church Foundation. Norman.

Polypod. Octagonal bowl. Early English, early thirteenth century.

Decoration

The font is rather defaced and the bowl is cracked down one face and has been repaired on the rim.

Each face has a wide trefoiled ogee arch with pointed trefoils in the spandrels. The faces were probably plain at first and cut later, probably during the fourteenth century. The bottom of the bowl is finished with a quirk.

The central stem has eight attached shafts each having Early English capitals the whole having been squared at the bottom and standing on a square base with chamfered top edge. The whole is mounted on a sub-base.

At the bases of alternate shafts are animal carvings very much defaced.

They may be:

North-east shaft: Crouching animal.

South-east: Animal (lion?) and leaf.

South-west: Two animals fighting.

North-west: Crouching animal.

O.S. Ref. No. 719 167.

ST. JOHN-THE-BAPTIST LITTLE MAPLESTEAD

Church Foundation: Decorated c1335 (believed built on site of previous Knights Templars church of twelfth century).

Monopod. Probably from earlier church. Square bowl with chamfered angles. Norman, c1080.

Decoration

The deep bowl was originally square but probably in the fifteenth century the corners were removed. The size of the bowl would indicate that it was used for total immersion in the Norman period.

The carving is rather crude the south and east faces each having two roughly carved scrolled volutes. The north face has two round-headed arches in low relief and the west face a rather antiquated form of St. Andrew's cross.

The bowl is mounted on a much later octagonal base which is hollow-chamfered to the pedestal which is also octagonal. The base is moulded and stands on an octagonal sub-base with priest's step.

The font originally stood against the south-west pier of the nave arcade but was probably removed to its present position during the 1851-57 restoration.

Cover

The cover is a flat wooden irregular octagon with iron ring handle. Modern.

O.S. Ref. No. 822 339

ALL SAINTS LITTLE TOTHAM

Church Foundation: Norman.

Monopod. Octagonal bowl. Perpendicular, fifteenth century.

Decoration

The rim of the bowl is chamfered and moulded.
The octagonal bowl is deep and displays various window tracery motifs of the Decorated and Perpendicular periods on the faces with three or four lights some having a transom.
The centre of the bowl is badly cracked and attempts have been made to repair it.
At the bottom of the bowl is a deeply cut quirk and moulding. The stem is octagonal and tapered to the moulded base.
The whole is mounted on a rectangular step having chamfered corners on the western side and incorporating a priest's step.

O.S. Ref. No. 884 103

ST. MARY-THE-VIRGIN LITTLE WAKERING

Church Foundation: Norman.

Monopod. Circular tub bowl. Norman, twelfth century.

Decoration

The circular tub-shaped bowl is tapered and plain with the exception of spurs or broaches in line with the angles of the octagonal base.
The rim shows scars where lid fastenings have been removed.
There is graffiti on the bowl.
The underside of the tub bowl has a small hollow chamfer to the very low octagonal pedestal on an octagonal two-stepped chamfered base which has low vertical sides. The pedestal and base is not considered to be contemporary with the bowl.

Cover

The cover is a flat wooden lid. In the centre is a square post. Four stop-chamfered convex cusped trusses rise from the lid meeting near the top of the post which ends in a pierced lozenge-shaped cross finial. Date of the cover is uncertain but could be seventeenth century.

O.S. Ref. No. 935 884

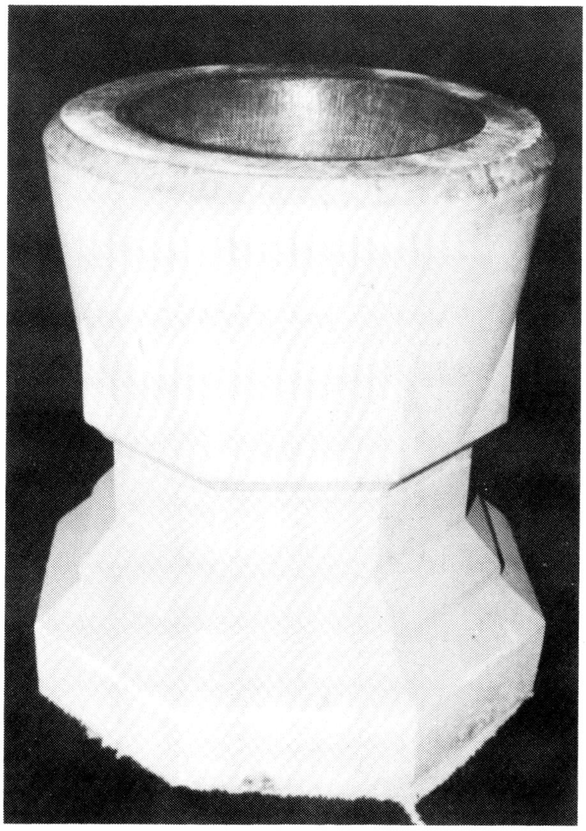

ST. PETER — LITTLE WARLEY

Church Foundation: Perpendicular (built on site of previous church – probably fourteenth century).

Monopod. Octagonal bowl. Classical, eighteenth century.

Decoration

The small octagonal alabaster bowl has a moulded edge with convex sides to an octagonal baluster pedestal having a moulded top and a ring moulding a little lower down. The small base is also octagonal and moulded.
The freestone pedestal is not believed to be contemporary with the bowl.

O.S. Ref. No. 603 887

ST. JOHN THE BAPTIST — LITTLE YELDHAM

Church Foundation: Early Perpendicular.

Monopod. Octagonal bowl. Perpendicular, early fifteenth century.

Decoration

East face: Small uncharged shield within a round-lobed quatrefoil within a circle.
North-east face: Fleuron within round-lobed quatrefoil within a circle.
North-face: Uncharged shield within round-lobed cinquefoil.
North-west face: Four scallop shells and disc within round-lobed quatrefoil within a circle.
West face: Uncharged shield within round-lobed quatrefoil within a circle.
South-west face: Fleuron within round-lobed quatrefoil within a circle.
South face: Uncharged shield within round-lobed quatrefoil within a circle.
South-east face: Five pointed star within round-lobed cinquefoil within a circle. (The mullet of the De Veres, Earls of Oxford of Castle Hedingham).
Underneath the bowl it is chamfered to pedestal.
The top of the modern octagonal pedestal is moulded but the centre part is plain.
The octagonal base is deep and has a hollow chamfer underneath which is a deep quirk. Under the quirk is a deep chamfer on top of stepped straight sides. The whole is mounted on a square step.

Cover

The flat wooden octagonal cover has a moulded edge. On top is a flat wrought iron equal armed fleurée cross each arm ending in a fleur-de-lis. In the centre is a ring handle. Modern.

O.S. Ref. No. 779 396

ST. MARY-THE-VIRGIN **MALDON**

Church Foundation: Norman.

Monopod. Octagonal bowl. Renaissance, c1700.

Decoration

The small bowl has a moulded rim with hollow chamfer and moulding under. The lower half has gadrooning.

The stem is octagonal with moulded base. It is of the Perpendicular period and probably formed part of the previous font.

The whole is mounted on a rectangular base which includes a priest's step.

O.S. Ref. No. 858 068

ST. MARGARET — MARGARET RODING

Church Foundation: Norman.

Monopod. Octagonal bowl. Perpendicular, fifteenth century.

Decoration

Each face has an uncharged shield within a round-lobed quatrefoil within a circle. The north shield is divided per pale by a vertical central ridge.
The underside of the bowl is chamfered to pedestal.
Lead lining to bowl has graffiti on rim.
Pedestal is octagonal set on an octagonal moulded base which is later. Each face of the pedestal has an upper and lower row of two light blank windows of the period (damaged in places) with variable traceried heads.
The rim of the bowl is damaged but has been partly repaired. Part of the hasp remains in situ.

Cover

The cover is a flat octagonal wooden lid with an iron equal armed fleurée cross with cable ring handle. Modern.

O.S. Ref. No. 598 120

ST. MARGARET — MARGARETTING

Church Foundation: Perpendicular

Monopod. Octagonal bowl. Perpendicular, fifteenth century.

Decoration

East face: Leaf in centre of round-lobed quatrefoil within a square.
North-east face: Crown in centre of round-lobed quatrefoil within a square.
North-face: Mitre in centre of round-lobed quatrefoil within a square.
North-west face: Mason's sign in centre of round-lobed quatrefoil within a square. (Square and Compasses).
West face: Face with tongue out in centre of round-lobed quatrefoil within a square.
South-west face: Five petalled flower in centre of round-lobed quatrefoil within a circle.
South-face: Rose in centre of round-lobed quatrefoil within a square.
South-east face: Foliate in centre of round-lobed quatrefoil within a square.
The octagonal stem has moulded top and bottom. Each face has deeply recessed lancet window form. Octagonal base with moulded top and trefoil on each face.
(See below)

Cover

Wooden octagonal boarded cover with moulded rim and ogee ribs terminating in an acorn finish.

O.S. Ref. No. 665 004

ST. ANDREW MARKS TEY

Church Foundation: Norman.

Monopod. Octagonal bowl. Perpendicular, late fifteenth century.

Decoration

A remarkable font made of oak with lead-lined bowl. One of the few in England. The bowl has eight traceried panelled faces divided by small buttresses each of which has an uncharged shield at the base.

Within the ogee arch on each face are carved throned figures and symbols of the Evangelists but these have suffered damage.

Between the bowl and pedestal five petalled roses are carved.

The octagonal pedestal has a dagger quatrefoil containing a five petalled rose with two trefoil headed lancets under between roll mouldings on each face.

The base is deeply hollow chamfered with a deep quirk at the bottom.

The whole is mounted on a stone sub-base chamfered on its top edge.

Cover

The octagonal oak cover is a boarded cone with moulded ribs and having at the base straight sides with moulding along the top and bottom. The cone terminates in a ball finial. Early seventeenth century.

O.S. Ref. No. 911 239

ST. MARY-THE-VIRGIN MATCHING

Church Foundation: Early English.

Monopod. Octagonal bowl. Purbeck marble, heavily whitewashed. Perpendicular, fifteenth century.

Decoration

East face: Round-lobed quatrefoil with rosette in centre.
North-east face: Round-lobed quatrefoil with small shield charged with a cross.
North face: Round-lobed quatrefoil with rosette on square in centre.
North-west face: Round-lobed quatrefoil with fleurette in centre.
West face: Round-lobed quatrefoil with square in centre.
South-west face: Round-lobed quatrefoil with cross in centre.
South face: Round-lobed quatrefoil with fleurette in centre.
South-east face: Round-lobed quatrefoil with small shield in centre charged with a chevron.
The underside of the bowl is concave with mouldings to lower edge of bowl and where it meets the pedestal.
The pedestal is octagonal and each face has lancet window forms except the west face which is blank.
There is roll moulding between pedestal and base which is deeply chamfered.

O.S. Ref. No. 525 120

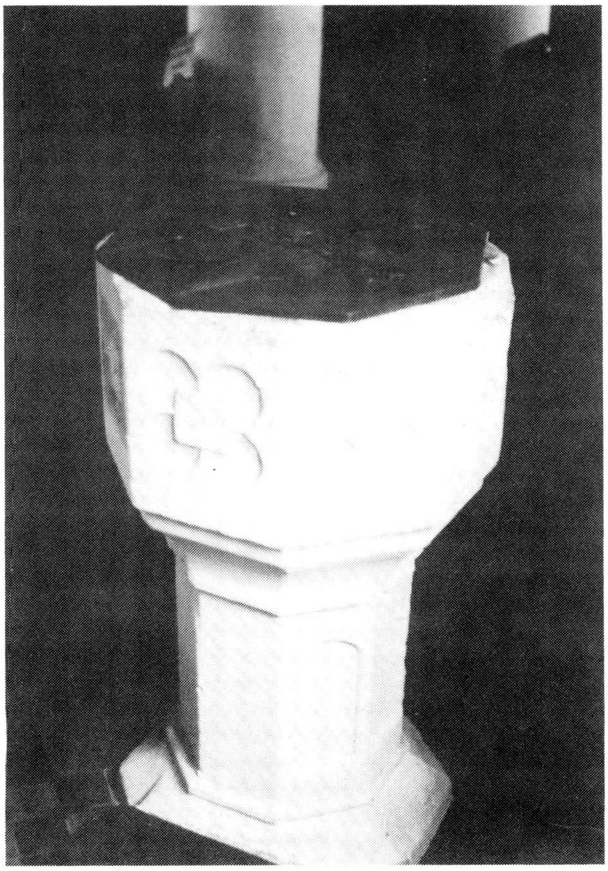

ST. MARY-THE-VIRGIN MORETON

Church Foundation: Early English.

Polypod. Square bowl. Purbeck marble. Transitional c1200.

Decoration

South face: Four fleur-de-lis.
East face: Four fleur-de-lis.
North face: Four shallow blank round-headed arches.
West face: Sun, moon and whorl.
The bowl is much mutilated and is mounted on a central drum pedestal with four Purbeck marble corner shafts on a square base with chamfered top edge. The bowl would appear to be much older than its mounting.

O.S. Ref. No. 537 071

ST. GILES MOUNTNESSING

Church Foundation: Early English.

Monopod. Octagonal bowl. Perpendicular, fifteenth century.

Decoration

The previous position of this font was directly opposite the south door but was translated to its present position in the south aisle. It came from Hutton Parish Church probably in 1873 when that church was rebuilt. The bowl is small and the faces are panelled and deeply recessed.

East face: A form of triquetra with ears of wheat.
North-east face: Acorns and leaves.
North face: Possibly square and compasses.
North-west face: Five petalled rosette.
West face: Patée cross.
South-west face: Fleurette.
South face: Patée cross — much damaged.
South-east face: Four leaves.

The under-side of the bowl is moulded and hollow-chamfered to the plain octagonal pedestal. The small base contains a hollow chamfer and the whole is mounted on a lipped octagonal sub-base with priest's step.

Cover

The cover is approximately nine feet in height and is in two sections.

The lower section is approximately four feet in height and has two hinged doors with pretty iron hinges.

The octagonal upper part commences with pierced leaf decoration with a hollow-chamfer under containing two fleurettes on each face and is a ribbed and boarded cone with a pierced pointed-lobed quatrefoil about half-way up each face. The cone terminates in a foliate based finial surmounted by a figure of the Blessed Virgin Mary and Child.

Inside the lower part the east, north-east and south-east faces each contain a window form of the period with the letters I.H.S. (Jesus). On the outside the east, north-west and south-east faces have carved on them the Latin words Aetrana far rum sanctis cuis in Gloria num prari but as they are in black letter they are difficult to distinguish.

O.S. Ref. No. 648 966

ALL SAINTS NAZEING

Church Foundation: Norman.

Monopod. Octagonal bowl. Perpendicular, fifteenth century.

Decoration

Each face has a round headed quatrefoil containing an uncharged shield.
The bowl is moulded at top and bottom.
Under the bowl there are four short uncarved corbels acting as supports.
The stem is Norman and round (drum shaped) with roll moulding near top.
Probably belonging to previous font.

O.S. Ref. No. 414 070

ST. MARY-THE-VIRGIN — NEWPORT

Church Foundation: Early English.

Polypod. Octagonal bowl. Early English, Thirteenth century.

Decoration

The bowl has a moulded rim.
Each face has a triangular headed arch over a trefoiled arch of unusual shape.
The stone pedestal is moulded at top and bottom and has eight marble supporting shafts having Early English capitals and bases. The whole is mounted on a modern step.

Cover

The cover is a flat wooden octagonal lid with central stem having four supporting columns with crockets rising to a foliated finial. Fifteenth century.

O.S. Ref. No. 521 342

Church Foundation: Norman.

Polypod. Square bowl, Purbeck type. Early English, thirteenth century.

Decoration

The square bowl has six shallow pointed arches on each side. A modern wooden top has been fitted to the rim.

The bowl is mounted on a modern large square pedestal having attached circular shafts with moulded bases of the Early English period at each angle.

The base is square with chamfered top and is two-stepped with priest's step. Is it original?

The whole has been painted with white paint!

O.S. Ref. No. 762 899

Church Foundation: Late fifteenth century, rebuilt eighteenth century.

Monopod. Octagonal bowl. Perpendicular, Fifteenth century.

Decoration

The octagonal bowl has concave faces carved in relief and there are remains of lid fastenings in the rim which is damaged on the south side.
East face: Shield charged with undulating lines (representing 'Regeneration'?)
North-east face: Large rosette.
North face: Shield charged with seven small recessed squares.
North-west face: Large rosette.
West face: Uncharged shield (hard against wall).
South-west face: Large rosette.
South face: Shield charged with four bars.
South-east face: Large rosette
The underside of the bowl is hollow-chamfered to half-round moulding.
The pedestal is short and octagonal.
The badly damaged base is square with indecipherable spurs at the angles.
Could it be much earlier than the font?

Cover

The cover is a round flat oak lid with chamfered edge having an equal armed wooden cross with knob handle in centre. Modern.

O.S. Ref. No. 850 972

Church Foundation: Decorated (built on site of earlier church).

Monopod. Square bowl, Barnack stone. Norman, late twelfth century

Decoration

Very plain straight-sided bowl having attached angle shafts moulded at top and bottom but much damaged.
Square pedestal base with moulded stop chamfers at each angle. The whole mounted on a rectangular base with priest's step. Modern. Part of original hasp remaining in rim of font.
This font is very similar to the one in Writtle church.

O.S. Ref. No. 046 580

ST. MARY-THE-VIRGIN NORTH SHOEBURY

Church Foundation: Early English (on site of previous church).

Polypod. Square bowl, Purbeck marble. Twelfth century bowl (probably either from previous church or the Cluniac Priory of Prittlewell).

Decoration

The Purbeck marble bowl is square and has plain rough sides. In each angle of the rim is a fleur-de-lis.

There are pieces of the lid fastenings remaining in the rim. The bowl is mounted on a large square pedestal with four plain attached circular shafts and a square base on the top of which is a circular pattern with a semi-circle at the point opposite each corner of the bowl.

The whole is mounted on a square sub-base.

The bowl quite evidently does not fit the supports which were obviously made for another bowl.

Cover

The cover is a circular flat wooden lid with a moulded edge. It has a circle of carved scroll work with semi-circles of chip carving. In a central circle is a form of equal armed cross having dart-shaped ends between which are four horseshoe and dart carvings. The cover has a central knob instead of the usual ring handle. It is dated 1892.

O.S. Ref. No. 929 862

ST. GILES AND ALL SAINTS — ORSETT

Church Foundation: Norman.

Monopod. Octagonal bowl. Perpendicular, c1500.

Decoration

The lower part of the rim is chamfered and the rim has been repaired.
East face: Charged shield in relief. 3 vertical lines, 2 having a small disc at each foot and centre line having a disc away from foot. (?Trinity).
North-east face: Rosette in relief.
North face: Charged shield in relief. Y-shaped cross.
North-west face: Rosette in relief.
West face: Charged shield in relief. Latin cross.
South-west face: Rosette in relief.
South face: Charged shield in relief. Y-shaped cross.
South-east face: Rosette in relief.
The underside of the bowl is deeply hollow-chamfered to pedestal.
The large octagonal pedestal has buttresses at alternate angles and the octagonal base has a chamfered top edge.
The whole is mounted on a large square stepped sub-base with chamfered angles on the western side.
Old lid fastenings are in situ on south and north faces.

Cover

The cover is a flat wooden lid having eight radiating iron spokes from central ring each spoke terminating in a fleur-de-lis. The lid has a cable ring handle. Modern.
Lying on the floor at the side of the font is what is described as a Saxon font but it would appear to be a holy water stoup.

O.S. Ref. No. 644 820

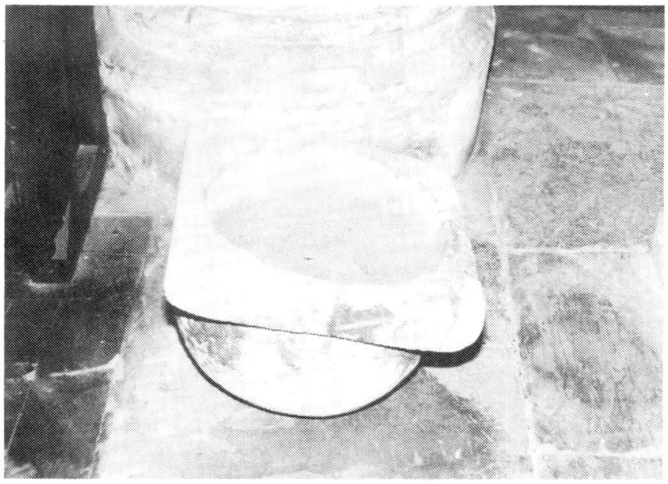

ST. MARY-THE-VIRGIN — OVINGTON

Church Foundation: Norman.

Monopod. Circular tub bowl. Norman, twelfth century.

Decoration

The plain circular bowl has a rough surface and is well worn.
The bowl is mounted on a square block of stone forming the base which is much later and into which carved fleurons, probably decorative features out of fragments of medieval dressings and tombs, have been inserted.
A priest's step is made from the base of a pier.

Cover, Seventeenth century.

The octagonal cover is a wooden boarded cone with plain ribs rising to a ball finial surmounted by a brass fleurée Latin cross. Originally the cover was polished wood but is now painted. The boarded part is coloured red, the ribs yellow (gold).

O.S. Ref. No. 763 426

ST. MARY-THE-VIRGIN PELDON

Church Foundation: Norman (on site of previous Anglo-Saxon church).

Polypod. Octagonal bowl. Norman, twelfth century.

Decoration

The bowl is octagonal with plain faces and a drum pedestal both of which are original.
The bowl is also supported by eight small shafts on a double chamfered octagonal base. The font has been much restored. The shafts and base replaced a brick base in the nineteenth century. Marks can be seen on the rim where lid fastenings used to be prior to the Reformation.

Cover

There is a flat octagonal wooden cover with an equal-armed wrought iron studded cross with central ring handle. Modern.

O.S. Ref. No. 989 168

ST. GEORGE

PENTLOW

Church Foundation: Early Norman.

Originally unmounted but now mounted on a square rubble and stone base. Square bowl. Norman, twelfth century.

Decoration

The large square bowl has attached angle colonnettes with scalloped cushion capitals and moulded bases.

The bowl is set against a wall thus revealing only three faces. Damage has been caused to the rim by the removal of lid fastenings.

East face: Sprays of acanthus leaves. Intersecting arcading. Interlacement.

South face: Cross. Stylised foliage. Fleurette. Linked rings.

West face: Star. Stylised foliage. Linked rings.

The bowl is mounted on a rubble base with stone quoins at two outside angles and includes a priest's step.

Cover

The cover is in two stages, the lower stage of the fifteenth century and the upper stage modern. Approximately seven feet in height.

The cover rests on the font and is composed of an octagonal lid of which only seven sides are visible. The lower stage is boarded and approximately three feet in height. Three of the sides are hinged to form a door giving access to the font. Each side forms a niche with nodding ogee arches and crocketed canopies the sides being divided by butresses. The top and bottom of this stage have bands of moulding. Much restoration has taken place.

The second stage, about four feet in height, is composed of open pointed cusped arches divided by buttresses with crocketed pinnacles. There is a central stem from which radiate eight boards crocketed on their acute edges and rising to a carved baluster finial.

O.S. Ref. No. 813 462

ANNUNCIATION OF THE BLESSED VIRGIN MARY — PRITTLEWELL

Church Foundation: Saxon.

Monopod. Octagonal bowl. Tudor, early sixteenth century.

Decoration

The bowl is unusual being a concave-faced octagon with under-side chamfered to the pedestal and is similar to Ashingdon and Faulkbourne fonts. Marks of lid fastenings may be seen on the rim.

Each face is recessed and contains:

East face: A charged shield. Chevron and 3 fleur-de-lis.

North-east face: Crucifixion.

North face: Half Tudor rose and half pomegranite (no doubt commemorating marriage of Henry VIII with Catherine of Aragon in 1509).

North-west face: Tudor rose.

West face: Blank.

South-west face: Tudor rose.

South face: Heart with crossed spears.

South-east face: Blank.

The faces of the bowl are not properly orientated to the east/west axis line of the church.

The pedestal is square with attached shafts at the angles having roll moulded capitals and bases. It may be earlier than the font but is more likely to be contemporary. The whole is mounted on an octagonal stepped sub-base with priest's step and has three rose tiles on the face of each step. Modern sub-base.

Cover

The cover is a flat wooden concave-sided octagonal lid with hollow chamfered edge in the centre of which is a raised circular piece. From the centre rises four radiating concave boards their inner edges being attached to a central turned baluster terminating in a further smaller circular piece on which is mounted an acorn finial. Modern.

A unique feature is a niche in the westernmost pier of the adjoining arcade. This niche was probably used to contain the salt or a bowl used by the sponsors for washing the hands or for small napkins all of which would be used during the baptismal service pre-Reformation.

This niche indicates where the font originally stood. In 1871/72 the font was moved to a position just inside the south door and later, in 1963/64 to its present position.

O.S. Ref. No. 877 868

ST. HELEN AND ST. GILES — RAINHAM

Church Foundation: Late Norman.

Monopod. Circular bowl, limestone. Norman, twelfth century.

Decoration

The bowl is circular with chamfered lower edge to pedestal.

Originally the bowl had two semi-circular projections level with the rim but one has been broken away. It is difficult to ascertain the exact use of these projections and it has been suggested that they were to provide a means for fastening down the cover of the font particularly as the sound projection retains some metal fittings. It is not felt that the projections were for this use as it would be an expensive method on an otherwise plain font and when many other medieval fonts had their lid fastenings in the rim. The projections were more likely for the support of an affusion basin or office book and this would have been effected by a metal rest. The other projection may have been used for the salt and candle which were accessories of the full western rite of baptism. The real purpose is open to conjecture.

It is very possible that the bowl originally stood either on the floor or on a low support. Later, in the fifteenth century it was placed on the present square pedestal which has niched buttresses at the angles, the four sides having recessed trefoiled head window forms.

The base is square with chamfered corners and chamfered top edge.

The whole is mounted on a large square sub-base with chamfered corners.

Cover

The cover is an octagonal stepped wooden lid with open ogee iron trusses forming a handle.

O.S. Ref. No. 526 822.

ST. MARY RAMSDEN BELLHOUSE

Church Foundation: Perpendicular.

Monopod. Octagonal bowl. Perpendicular, fifteenth century.

Decoration

The octagonal bowl is plain with the exception of the underside which is moulded.
The pedestal is octagonal and plain.
The base is octagonal and has a moulded chamfered top to stepped vertical sides separated by a hollow-chamfer. The lower part of the base has been cut-off on the western side to incorporate a priest's step which is modern. Part of the base has been damaged. The whole font has been painted.

Cover

The cover is a wooden octagonal lid in the centre of which is an octagonal metal plate from which arises on each side a wrought iron scroll, the eight scrolls terminating with a fleurette having delightfully shaped petals. This lid replaces a graceful seventeenth century cover which would appear to have been present in 1954 (Pevsner).

O.S. Ref. No. 719 943

ALL SAINTS RAYNE

Church Foundation: The Norman church which replaced a Saxon church was rebuilt in 1840 with the exception of the fine Tudor brick tower built c1510.

Monopod. Octagonal bowl. Decorated, Fourteenth century (restored).

Decoration

The rim is embattled and moulded and underneath is a band of naturalistic foliage of leaf and grape.
Each face has a crocketed moulded ogee canopy above which there are trefoiled-head window forms in the spandrels.
Within the ogee canopies are cusped recesses each cusp terminating with a fleurette. The recesses are surrounded by fleurettes and the faces are separated by buttresses.
Each ogee canopy contains:
East face: Shield charged with a cross.
North-east face: Winged bull — symbol of the Evangelist St. Luke.
North-face: Shield charged with I.H.S. (Monogram of Jesus).
North-west face: Eagle — symbol of the Evangelist St. John.
West face: Shield charged with the dove of peace.
South-west face: Winged man — symbol of the Evangelist St. Matthew.
South face: Shield charged with Latin form of Hand of God in blessing.
South-east face: Winged lion — symbol of Evangelist St. Mark.
The bottom of the bowl is chamfered with bosses of fleurettes at the points of intersection beneath the buttresses.
The faces of the octagonal stem are separated by shafts with moulded capitals and bases of the period. Each face contains a window form of the period.
The base is chamfered and moulded and the whole is mounted on a rectangular plinth with priest's step.
Affixed to the base on the east side is a small coat of arms in a circle probably the arms of the donor.

Cover

The cover is a flat wooden lid having a tall wrought-iron Latin cross in the centre from which radiate four wrought-iron scrolls containing leaf patterns. Modern.
In the corner of the western end of the south wall is a plain seventeenth century font not now used.

O.S. Ref. No. 733 229

ALL SAINTS RICKLING

Church Foundation: Early English (Probably on site of pre-conquest church).

Monopod. Octagonal bowl, limestone. Perpendicular, early fifteenth century.

Decoration

The faces are plain with the exception of the east face which has a recessed round-headed trefoil within a circle (probably representing the Holy Trinity). In each corner of the face is a small lozenge-shaped decoration.

On the rim may be seen the scars where the original cover fastenings have been removed. The holes have been very neatly filled in with stone.

The stem is octagonal and may be earlier than the bowl. It is moulded at the top and has a two tier base. The top tier is octagonal with chamfered edge and the lower tier is square but cut into octagonal shape with chamfered top edge leaving spurs to corners.

O.S. Ref. No. 498 315

ST. MARY AND ALL SAINTS RIVENHALL

Church Foundation: Anglo-Saxon.

Originally monopod. Octagonal bowl. Decorated, early fourteenth century.

Decoration

The present font is Victorian and replaced an early fourteenth century font in the mid-nineteenth century. The medieval font is, regretfully, in pieces, part of it having been used as a bird bath in the old rectory garden. The majority of the pieces are now piled in a corner of a shed in the churchyard. It is understood that they were removed from the rectory garden in the 1970s and placed in the chancel of the church but have since been removed to their present position. It is hoped that the pieces will eventually be fitted together and the result placed back in the church.

The bowl and pedestal were, it is believed, octagonal, the bowl having plain faces with moulding on the underside and the pedestal having niches on each face.

It is interesting to note that following recent archaeological investigations it has been established that the site of the church has been occupied since before Roman times and part of the remains of a Roman villa lies beneath the chancel. Prior to the building of the present church there was an early Christian Saxon timber church lying to the east and being partly under the present sanctuary.

O.S. Ref. No. 827 178

ST. PETER ROYDON

Church Foundation: Early English.

Polypod. Octagonal bowl. Decorated, c1300.

Decorated

Faces plain but in the four diagonals are four heads, possibly four workmen wearing hats with rolled-up brims.
Supports and stem have roll moulding at top and bottom.
Rim of bowl has been much repaired.

Cover

The cover is made of oak in the shape of an enclosed octagonal cone having crocketed straight ribs between the faces ending in an octagonal finial.

O.S. Ref. No. 407 103

ST. MARY — RUNWELL

Church Foundation: Early English (built on site of earlier church)

Monopod. Octagonal bowl. Perpendicular, early fifteenth century.

Decoration

The octagonal bowl is badly damaged on rim and faces. There are marks where the lid fastenings have been removed.
The faces of the bowl are plain and the underside is inset and rounded to the short plain octagonal pedestal.
The octagonal base is deeply hollow-chamfered to shallow vertical sides.

Cover

The cover is a plain octagonal wooden lid with a central circular iron plate with ring handle — Modern.

O.S. Ref. No. 754 944

ST. MARY-THE-VIRGIN   SAFFRON WALDEN

Church Foundation: Early English.

Monopod. Octagonal bowl, Ketton stone. Perpendicular, fifteenth century.

Decoration

Pointed-lobed quatrefoils on each face with foliates in centre except on north face which has an uncharged shield.

Underside of bowl is moulded.

Octagonal pedestal with foliates at top and trefoiled head lancet on each face and each panel having a foliate at the base.

The base is moulded and the whole is mounted on a sub-base with priest's step.

Round the top of the bowl are the following carved letters – MANEAT VSVS MEI, TOLLATUR ABVSVS – MAY THE USE OF ME ABIDE, MAY MY ABUSE BE DONE AWAY WITH.

These words were added in the nineteenth century.

The font originally had many coats of paint which have been removed.

Cover

The cover is an octagonal lid with moulded edge having eight radiating trusses rising from the angles and meeting at the head of a centre baluster-shaped post just below the finial which is composed of a ball surmounted with a cross.

Modern.

O.S. Ref. No. 536 388

ST. PETER AND ST. PAUL ST. OSYTH

Church Foundation, Norman.

Monopod. Octagonal bowl. Late Tudor, sixteenth century.

Decoration

East face: Defaced crucifix in octfoil.
North-east face: Scourge in circle within round-lobed quatrefoil.
North face: Octfoil containing shield charged with three crowns (Armorial bearings of Abbey and arms of Kingdom of East Anglia).
North-west face: Round-lobed quatrefoil having floriated cusps with head of St. Osyth in centre framed in leaves.
West face: An angel bearing a shield carrying soul of St. Osyth to Paradise.
South-west face: Round-lobed quatrefoil with head of St. John-the-Baptist on charger in centre.
South face: Octfoil with shield in centre charged with key of St. Peter and sword of St. Paul.
South-east face: Round-lobed quatrefoil having a circle containing Sacred Heart in centre.
The underside of the bowl is concave and is decorated on:
East face: Leaf design.
North-east face: Leaf design.
North face: Leaf design.
North-west face: Leaf design.
West face: Shield charged with a Latin cross.
South-west face: Leaf design.
South face: Looped quadrate cross.
South-east face: Leaf design.
The pedestal has trefoiled head lancets on each face.
The base has a moulded chamfered edge with priest's step.

Cover

The cover is modern and is composed of an octagonal lid with a boarded and ribbed cone with a St. James's cross finial. Each panel contains a quatrefoil with fleurette in centre.
Each face of the base is carved with four lozenge-shapes each containing a pointed-lobed quatrefoil.

O.S. Ref. No. 123 156

ST. ANDREW   SANDON

Church Foundation: Norman.

Monopod. Octagonal bowl. Decorated, fourteenth century.

Decoration

The octagonal bowl has plain faces. The flat topped rim is badly damaged but partly repaired and there are remains of lid fastenings.
The underside of the bowl is well moulded and chamfered to a half-round moulding.
The octagonal pedestal is short and plain.
From the pedestal the octagonal base is hollow-chamfered to vertical sides and there is a small priest's step.

Cover

The cover is a flat octagonal oak lid with hollow-chamfered edge bearing four radiating trusses rising from between the alternate angles and attached to an octagonal central post which terminates in an acorn finial. Modern.

O.S. Ref. No. 743 048

ST. ANDREW

SHALFORD

Church Foundation: Decorated.

Monopod. Hexagonal bowl. Perpendicular, fifteenth century.

Decoration

The hexagonal bowl has a moulded rim.
North-east face: Two round-lobed quatrefoils each within a circle and containing charged shields. The circles are divided by a lancet window form. The left shield is of the De Vere family and the right shield possible the Littleton family but this is uncertain.
South-east face: Three trefoils side by side each trefoil having two pointed and one round lobe.
South face: Two round-lobed quatrefoils each within a circle and containing charged shields. The circles are divided by a lancet window form. The left shield is of the Mortimer family and the right of the Fitzwalter family.
South-west face: Two pointed-lobed quatrefoils divided by a lancet window form.
North-west face: Two round-lobed quatrefoils each within a circle and containing charged shields. The circles are divided by a lancet window form. The left shield is of the Scales family and the right is of the Coggeshall family.
North face: Three trefoils side by side.
Underside of bowl is chamfered to pedestal.
The pedestal is hexagonal each face having two varied traceried lancets. Each face is divided by a buttress culminating in a set-off.
Base of pedestal is moulded.
The whole stands on a rectangular stone base.

Cover

The hexagonal flat wooden lid has battlemented sides with a stepped cross of Glory in centre.

O.S. Ref. No. 724 293

ST. MARY THE VIRGIN SHEERING

Church Foundation: Norman.

Polypod. Square bowl, Purbeck Marble. Norman, twelfth century.

Decoration

The square bowl has shallow blank arcading consisting of five plain round-headed arches on each face.
The bowl is badly worn and has been pieced together.
The supports are missing and the bowl is now supported on land drainage pipes.
This font is in the choir vestry on the south side of the west tower. It was found in the rectory garden.
The present font in use in the church is a modern copy of the Norman font. The bowl is supported on a round central pedestal with four round detached corner shafts on a square base.

O.S. Ref. No. 509 137

ST. MARY THE VIRGIN SHENFIELD

Church Foundation: Early English (major restoration and extension in 15th century)

Monopod. Octagonal bowl, Caen stone called Palotte. Perpendicular, c1390.

Decoration

The rim of the bowl is much damaged.
East face: Round-lobed quatrefoil in circle with foliated head in centre (Green Man).
North-east face: Round-lobed quatrefoil in circle with fleurette in centre.
North face: Round-lobed quatrefoil in circle with cat head in centre.
North-west face: Round-lobed quatrefoil in circle with fleurette in centre.
West face: Round-lobed quatrefoil in circle with fleurette in centre.
South-west face: Round-lobed quatrefoil in circle with foliate in centre.
South-face: Round-lobed quatrefoil with head in centre.
South-east face: Round-lobed quatrefoil in circle with a patée fitched cross in a lozenge in centre.
The underside is moulded with hollow-chamfer and half-round moulding to octagonal pedestal.
The pedestal is late nineteenth century having on each side a panelled trefoiled head window form containing various foliate formations.
The base has a half-round moulding with hollow-chamfer and quirk.
The whole is mounted on a small octagonal sub-base.

Cover

The cover is a round flat oak lid with iron ring handle. Modern c1949.

NOTE: This font has a rather unusual history. It was installed c1390 and at some time was mounted on a wooden shaft which was in use by 1856. Prior to the restoration work of 1862/63 the font was moved to the churchyard where it was occasionally used for baptism.

In the late 1870's the Rector the Rev. T. P. Ferguson decided that the church should have a 'proper' font made of English oak but this idea was abandoned and he then decided to have a marble font. The Rector visited the quarries at Carrera in Italy and a font was ordered. On arrival a flaw was found and the Rector refused to accept it. A further font was made and installed in the church in 1878 at a cost of £123.

Canon W. Quennell became Rector and in 1895 a friend, the Rev. F. W. Ragg, Rector of Marsworth, Buckinghamshire, visited him. The friend, an amateur sculpture and stonemason of considerable skill, on seeing the old stone font, now in the Rectory garden, became concerned that it should be left exposed to the weather. Mr. Ragg asked whether he might restore if for use in his church. Eventually it was bought and taken to Marsworth where renovation work was carried out to the basin and a completely new pedestal provided. Some of the Shenfield parishioners wished for the return of their font, which had been removed without a Faculty, and made efforts for its return. In 1949 this was arranged and it was erected by the south door and a new cover of English oak was provided at a cost of £70.

O.S. Ref. No. 605 952

ST. LEONARD SOUTHMINSTER

Church Foundation: Norman.

Monopod. Octagonal bowl. Perpendicular, fifteenth century.

Decoration

The font is well designed but the octagonal bowl is unusually small being only two feet in diameter.

Each face of the bowl has a fleurette within a round-lobed quatrefoil. The spandrels are floriated.

The underside edge is moulded with hollow-chamfer to pedestal. The faces of the chamfer have a fleurette on each face.

The octagonal pedestal has a cinquefoiled head window form with a round-lobed quatrefoil having a fleurette in the centre underneath on each face.

The top edge of the base is hollow-chamfered with fleurette on each face dividing the chamfer from the straight sides of the base is roll moulding. Each side of the base has a round-lobed quatrefoil supported on either side by a small conquefoiled head window form. The bottom of the base is moulded.

The whole is mounted on an octagonal sub-base.

Cover

Victorian, nineteenth century.

The octagonal cover has a flat wooden base from which rises tall sides with buttreeses having floriated pinnacles at the angles. Each side is panelled.

1. Round-lobed quatrefoil with a shield in centre charged XNI (Jesus Christ Victor).
2. Round-lobed quatrefoil with pointed ovals in spandrels. In centre of quatrefoil is a shield charged with letter S.
3. Round-lobed quatrefoil with a shield in centre charged with letter L.
4. Round-lobed quatrefoil with pointed ovals in spandrels. In centre are the letters IHS (C) (Jesus – Saviour).
5. Round-lobed quatrefoil with a shield in centre charged with a Dove (Peace) (Holy Spirit).
6. Round-lobed quatrefoil with pointed ovals in spandrels. In centre of quatrefoil is a shield charged with chain links (Trinity).
7. Round-lobed quatrefoil with a shield in centre charged with a fish (Early Christian symbol – Christ).
8. Round-lobed quatrefoil with pointed ovals in spandrels. In centre of quatrefoil is a shield charged with a Latin cross.

Rising from the sides is an eight-sided enclosed cone with the sides variously carved with round-lobed quatrefoils, pointed quatrefoils and a cross in a circle on two of the sides. The cone terminates with a floriated finial.

O.S. Ref. No. 959 997

ST. PETER SOUTH WEALD

Church Foundation: Norman.

Monopod. Octagonal bowl. Classical, 1662.

Decoration

The small octagonal hemi-spherical type bowl has a moulded rim with moulding where it meets the pedestal finished with a half-round moulding.
The pedestal is octagonal with heavy acanthus leaves sprouting from the base.
The base is moulded and chamfered almost to floor level.
The pedestal has the initials TD and date 1662 engraved upon it.
It is peculiar that the bowl drainage hole has its exit just under the moulding at the top of the pedestal.

Cover

The tall octagonal oak cover is conical and probably eighteenth century. The angles are buttressed with foliate crockets. Between the buttresses the cover is boarded, decorated with three round-lobed trefoils, three lancet window forms and a round-lobed quatrefoil, all pierced.

The lower part has short buttresses at the angles with two panels between the buttresses. Each panel contains a blank round-lobed trefoil and the panels are battlemented.

The cover rises to a foliate finial which hooks on to a banded metal ball painted blue with red band surmounted by a brass or gilt dove. The cover is hoisted by an iron chain counterpoised by a decorative iron weight.

O.S. Ref. No. 571 939

ALL SAINTS SPRINGFIELD

Church Foundation: Norman.

Monopod. Square bowl. Early English, mid thirteenth century.

Decoration

East face: Stiff leaf scrolls.
North face: Two large rosettes.
West face: Two large rosettes.
South face: Two large rosettes.
The rim is moulded.
Each corner has stiff-leaf carving on the angle.
In between the rosettes there is stiff-leaf and running from each corner to the pedestal is an acanthus leaf.
The surface of the drum pedestal is plain but the top edge has half-round moulding and the bottom edge water-holding moulding. The pedestal is mounted on a square base which has connected stiff-leaf spurs, the whole being mounted on a square sub-base having a moulded top edge and priest's step.
The whole of the decoration is very fine and in good condition.
This font is considered to be the best of the Early English fonts in Essex.

O.S. Ref. No. 719 080

ST. PETER AND ST. THOMAS STAMBOURNE

Church Foundation: Norman.

Monopod. Octagonal bowl. Perpendicular, early fifteenth century.

Decoration

The octagonal bowl has a chamfered edge and the faces are deeply recessed. The underside of the bowl has cherub heads at each angle and a fleurette on each face.

East face: Round-lobed octfoil in circle.

North-east face: Uncharged shield within an octfoil where round and pointed foils alternate.

North face: Round-lobed octfoil in circle.

North-west face: Uncharged shield within an octfoil where round and pointed foils alternate.

West face: Round-lobed octfoil in circle.

South-west face: Uncharged shield within an octfoil where round and pointed foils alternate.

South face: Round-lobed octfoil in circle.

South-east face: Uncharged shield within an octfoil where round and pointed foils alternate.

The octagonal pedestal has a different traceried and transomed window form on each face. The octagonal base is composed of two hollow-chamfered steps and the whole is mounted on a deep octagonal sub-base with priest's step.

O.S. Ref. No. 721 388

ST. MARGARET-OF-ANTIOCH STANFORD-LE-HOPE

Church Foundation: Norman.

Polypod. Octfoil bowl, Purbeck marble. Early English, thirteenth century.

Decoration

The plain octfoil bowl is very mutilated and it would appear that the top half has been joined to the lower half. Underneath each of the foils is a quirk.
The bowl is supported on a circular central pedestal and eight plain detached circular shafts having circular bases.
The base is square with rounded angles and is very worn.
The whole is mounted on a square sub-base with chamfered angles.

Cover

The boarded cover has a flat square wooden base from which rise eight ogee crocketed ribs to form an octagon terminating in a bud and foliated finial.
Seventeenth century.

O.S. Ref. No. 684 823

ST. MARGARET — STANFORD RIVERS

Church Foundation: Norman.

Polypod. Octagonal bowl, Purbeck type, Barnack stone. Early English, c1200.

Decoration

The large octagonal bowl has two shallow blank pointed arches on each face.
The rim has been badly damaged but partly repaired.
The bowl is supported by a short circular central pedestal with eight short circular shafts mounted on a large octagonal base the top edge of which is slightly chamfered.
The whole has been painted white.

Cover

The cover is a plain thin boarded lid with a short central turned baluster handle. Varnished. Age unknown.

O.S. Ref. No. 534 009

ST. MARY-THE-VIRGIN STANSTED MOUNTFITCHET

Church Foundation: Norman.

Monopod. Circular bowl, Barnack stone. Early English, early thirteenth century.

Decoration

The bowl has course angle volutes with cable moulding between bowl and pedestal.
The drum pedestal has a water-holding moulding at its base.
The whole is mounted on a later rectangular stone step which has cut-off corners on the east side.

Cover, Seventeenth century.

Wooden octagonal boarded cover with moulded rim and ogee ribs terminating in a floriated cross.

O.S. Ref. No. 521 242

ST. ALBRIGHT — STANWAY

Church Foundation: Early Norman.

Monopod. Octagonal bowl. Perpendicular, Fifteenth century.

Decoration

The rim of the octagonal bowl is badly damaged where lid fastenings have been removed.
Four of the deeply recessed panelled faces represent the Holy Sacrament.
East face: A chalice surrounded by rays of glory.
North-east face: Uncharged shield.
North face: A chalice within which is the Sacred Host surrounded by rays of glory.
North-west face: Uncharged shield.
West face: A chalice surrounded by rays of glory.
South-west face: Uncharged shield.
South face: A chalice surrounded by rays of glory.
South-east face: Uncharged shield.
The faces are very mutilated, probably caused by the Puritans, and it is extremely difficult to decide whether all the four chalices originally contained the Sacred Host and were identical or whether, perhaps, three of the chalices contained some other emblem.

The underside of the bowl is moulded and hollow-chamfered to pedestal which is octagonal with plain faces.
The top of the small octagonal base is hollow-chamfered and moulded and the whole is mounted on a large octagonal sub-base with priest's step.
The font originally stood close to the north door but was moved c1968.

Cover – 1955

The cover has a flat octagonal lid with moulded edge. Above the lid rise short sides with pinnacled buttresses at each angle. Alternate sides are pierced with a round-lobed quatrefoil in a circle with a fleurette in the centre and a foliate surmounting the quatrefoil. The other panels are similar but in the centre of each is an emblem of the Evangelists i.e. winged man, winged lion, winged bull and eagle.
From the sides rises a cone with concave crocketed ribs with boarded sides to a foliated finial.
The cover is counterpoised with an iron cylinder filled with cement.

O.S. Ref. No. 971 232

ST. MARY　　STAPLEFORD TAWNEY

Church Foundation, Early English (probably on site of previous church)

Monopod. Square. Early nineteenth century.

Decoration

The small square bowl is formed in the shape of a Norman cushion capital with half-round moulding where it joins a circular shaft pedestal. The pedestal has two stepped hollow-chamfers at the bottom where it joins a small square base having chamfered corners. The whole is mounted on a square sub-base.

Cover

Date not known but probably eighteenth century.

The wooden cover is square with moulded edge but was obviously not made for this font. The sides are boarded and rise in a double ogee shape to an acorn shaped finial.

O.S. Ref. No. 533 009

ST. MARY THE VIRGIN — STEBBING

Church Foundation: Decorated.

Monopod. Octagonal bowl. Decorated, fourteenth century.

Decorated

Plain sides to bowl.
Slightly moulded rim with moulding under bowl.
Stem octagonal each face having a cinquefoiled head recess.
Square base with hollow chamfered edge having small spurs at each angle. The whole mounted on rectangular sub-base with priest's step at west end.
It is believed that this font was encased but there is no remaining evidence. This may account for the faces of the bowl being plain and in such good condition.

Cover

The cover is made of oak in the shape of an enclosed octagonal cone having foliated crocketed straight ribs between the faces rising to a poppyhead finial. Each face has a round lobed quatrefoil within a circle surmounted by a foliation. The top of the base has foliation cresting and the bottom is moulded. Around the base are the pierced words 'Suffer little children to come unto me'. Modern.

O.S. Ref. No. 664 240

ST. LAURENCE STEEPLE

Church Foundation: Victorian (Materials from previous medieval church reused).

Monopod. Octagonal bowl. Perpendicular, fifteenth century.

Decoration

The rim of the octagonal bowl has been badly damaged and repaired in places. The bowl is shallow and has uncharged shields carved in relief on the east, north, west and south faces the remaining faces being plain.

The edge of the rim is lipped and the underside of the bowl is moulded and chamfered to the pedestal.

The pedestal is large and octagonal and has attached supporting shafts with capitals and bases at alternate angles.

The base is octagonal with hollow-chamfered top edge. The whole is mounted on an octagonal sub-base with priest's step.

The pedestal and base are modern and the bowl was re-erected in the early part of this century after having been found by the then Rector in the village where it had been used as a cattle trough.

Cover

The cover is a round oak lid with an equal armed iron cross with fleur-de-lis ends and central ring handle. Modern.

O.S. Ref. No. 934 030.

ST. MARY THE VIRGIN — STEEPLE BUMPSTEAD

Church Foundation: Norman.

Monopod. Octagonal bowl. Perpendicular, fifteenth century.

Decoration:

The octagonal bowl has a recessed round-lobed quatrefoil within a circle with uncharged shield in centre on each face with the exception of the west face which is plain.
Portions of the lid fastenings remain in situ.
The bowl joins the plain octagonal pedestal with a half-round moulding.
The octagonal base is chamfered on the top edge.
Both the pedestal and base would appear to be much later.
In Victorian times the font stood under the tower but was later moved to its present position. The fact that the font was originally in the tower where there is no western entrance probably accounts for the plain west face.

Cover

The cover is composed of an octagonal boarded wooden lid having a moulded edge. Eight moulded concave ribs rise from each angle to an acorn finial. In the centre of the lid is a small baluster handle. Modern.

O.S. Ref. No. 410 679.

ST. MARY — STIFFORD

Church Foundation: Norman.

Polypod. Square bowl. Early English, thirteenth century.

Decoration

The square bowl has plain slightly tapered sides and has been much repaired. There are remains of old lid fastenings in rim.

The base of the bowl is inset and circular supported on a trefoiled central pedestal with four detached corner shafts having moulded capitals and bases.

The central pedestal has its own base. The corner shafts have their capitals attached to the base of the bowl and their bases to the pedestal base.

The small base is square and the font is against the west side of the central pier in the south arcade.

The whole is mounted on a square sub-base with the western side having rounded corners.

O.S. Ref. No. 605 803

ALL SAINTS **STOCK**

Church Foundation: Decorated

Monopod. Octagonal bowl. Perpendicular, early fifteenth century.

Decoration

The octagonal bowl has plain faces which are damaged and the underside is moulded to the pedestal.

The pedestal is a tall plain octagonal on a hollow-chamfered short straight-sided base.

Cover

The cover is modern by Francis Stephens and replaced a previous seventeenth century cover.

It is in the form of a coronal symbolising the Crown of All Saints who began their Christian lives in the waters of Baptism.

O.S. Ref. No. 987 688

ST. PETER AND ST. PAUL STONDON MASSEY

Church Foundation: Early Norman.

Monopod. Octagonal bowl. Perpendicular, c.1400.

Decoration

The octagonal bowl has a chamfered rim edge with hollow chamfer under. The panelled faces are deeply recessed each having a round-lobed quatrefoil with a foliate in the centre.
The bottom edge is deeply moulded to a plain octagonal pedestal.
The base has a half-round moulding at the top with a wide hollow-chamfer under and a further hollow-chamfer to short vertical sides.
The whole is mounted on a large octagonal sub-base with priest's step.

Cover

The cover is a flat wooden octagonal lid with wrought iron equal armed cross with central ring handle. Modern.

O.S. Ref. No. 573 016

Church Foundation: Perpendicular

Monopod. Octagonal bowl. Perpendicular, late fifteenth century.

Decoration

The small octagonal bowl has a hollow-chamfered rim with a deep moulded underside.
Each face is recessed and contains a round-lobed quatrefoil within a circle.
The tall pedestal is octagonal and each face has a recessed trefoiled head window form.
The stepped base is topped with a hollow-chamfer with round edged quirk.
There is a priest's step attached.

O.S. Ref. No. 834 994

ST. MARY STRETHALL

Church Foundation: Anglo Saxon.

Polypod. Octagonal bowl. Norman, late twelfth century.

Decoration

The deep bowl would originally have been square but later (? thirteenth century) re-cut into a tapered octagonal shape. This is evidenced by the thickness of the bowl and that the cutting has left part of the shaft capitals exposed. The surface of the bowl is plain and roughly cut.

Where the rim has been damaged by the removal of the lid fastenings the damaged portions have been filled with pieces of stone.

The central stem is square with chamfered corners. There are four short supporting shafts the north-east and south-west are round with cushion capitals and square bases having chamfered angles. The north-west and south-east shafts are square with chamfered angles with square capitals chamfered at the angles and square bases having chamfered angles.

The base is octagonal and the whole is mounted on an octagonal sub-base with priest's step.

Cover

The cover is a plain circular flat wooden lid with iron ring handle. Modern.

O.S. Ref. No. 485 398

ALL SAINTS SUTTON

Church Foundation: Norman.

Polypod. Square bowl, Purbeck type. Early English, thirteenth century.

Decoration

The rim of the bowl is damaged and the bowl is cracked vertically in three places being repaired with lead insets on the rim.
Each face has five pointed shallow arcades.
The bowl is mounted on a central round stem with four corner shafts all having thirteenth century style capitals and bases on a square base. All this is modern.
The whole is mounted on a square stepped sub-base with cut-off corners and priest's step.

O.S. Ref. No. 888 893

HOLY TRINITY TAKELEY

Church Foundation: Norman.

Monopod, Modern. Octagonal bowl and pedestal.

Cover – Fifteenth century

Tall, six feet, lavish crocketed ogee arches with buttresses and flying buttresses and with tier upon tier of crocketed pinnacles. Much restored. Counterpoised by a simple stone.

O.S. Ref. No. 556 216

ST .EDMUND KING AND MARTYR TENDRING

Church Foundation: Early English.

Monopod. Octagonal bowl. Tudor, Sixteenth century.

Decoration

The rim of the octagonal bowl is bevelled and has been varnished.
The square panelled faces are elaborately carved with foliage and uncharged shields.
East face: Uncharged shield surrounded with fruit and foliage.
North-east face: Pomegranate (eternal life) surrounded with foliage.
North-face: uncharged shield surrounded with fruit and foliage.
North-west face: Pomegranate surrounded with foliage.
West face: Uncharged shield surrounded with fruit and foliage.
South-west face: Pomegranate surrounded with foliage.
South face: Uncharged shield surrounded with fruit and foliage.
South-east face: Pomegranate surrounded by fruit and foliage.
The underside of the bowl is moulded and under which is a curious pattern which is probably meant to represent water (see Thorrington).
The short octagonal pedestal has deeply recessed cinquefoil headed panels to a moulded and chamfered base.

Cover

The cover is a flat wooden octagonal lid with an equal armed iron cross having bifurcated ends and cable ring handle in centre. Modern.

O.S. Ref. No. 143 242

ALL SAINTS — TERLING

Church Foundation: Early English.

Polypod. Octagonal bowl, Purbeck marble. Early English, thirteenth century.

Decoration

The octagonal bowl has two shallow pointed arches on each face.
The rim has been badly damaged but repaired in places.
Round the bowl is a deep score mark. It would be interesting to know how the mark came to be there.
The bowl is mounted on an octagonal central pedestal and eight round detached angle shafts all with Early English style capitals and bases and mounted on a square stepped base with chamfered top edge. Modern.

Cover

The cover is a circular lid on which is mounted a shallow enclosed octagonal sided drum each side having two floriates carved in relief. From the angles of the drum rise pierced concave trusses affixed to a central baluster. The top of the trusses is finished with crenellation. Modern.

O.S. Ref. No. 774 148

ST. JOHN-THE-BAPTIST THAXTED

Church Foundation: Decorated.

It is not possible to see the font but it is presumed to be of the Perpendicular period.
The font is completely encased in wood, the case being fixed to the floor.
It is provided with doors hinged to open when the font is required for use and is octagonal in shape.
There are two tiers of traceried panels.
The case is surmounted by an elaborately carved cover having buttresses and canopies topped by a crocketed finial.
The case and cover are late fifteenth century.
It would appear that in 1922 the font and cover were situate a little to the south of the nave, immediately under the western arch of the south arcade, and later re-positioned in their present position.
NOTE. There is one other encased font at Littlebury.

O.S. Ref. No. 611 310.

ST. LEONARD THE HYTHE, COLCHESTER

Church Foundation: Decorated.

Monopod. Octagonal bowl. Perpendicular, fifteenth century.

Decoration

The rim of the octagonal bowl has been damaged but repaired in places. The faces have large square recessed panels.
East face: Leaves with fruit in centre.
North-east face: Round-lobed quatrefoil with uncharged shield in centre.
North face: Chalice and Host with rays of glory.
North-west face: Round-lobed quatrefoil with uncharged shield in centre.
West face: Leaves with fruit in centre.
South-west face: Round-lobed quatrefoil with uncharged shield in centre.
South face: Agnus Dei in rays of glory.
South-east face: Round-lobed quatrefoil with uncharged shield in centre.
The underside of the bowl is shallow hollow-chamfered to moulding and then deeply hollow-chamfered to half-round moulding at top of pedestal.
The octagonal pedestal has a trefoil headed window form on each face.
The octagonal base has a hollow-chamfered top edge to shallow vertical sides.
The whole is mounted on a seven sided sub-base with priest's step.

Cover

The tall cover has an octagonal box base with moulded top and bottom edges. On the top of the base is a short moulded cone having four trusses. Rising from the trusses is an octagonal column with four crocketed ribs supported by four flying buttresses having pinnacles and crockets. The whole rises to a large foliate finial. Victorian.

O.S. Ref. No. 006 244

ST. MICHAEL THE ARCHANGEL THEYDON MOUNT

Church Foundation: Early Renaissance, seventeenth century.

Monopod, wall mounted. Small rectangular basin of black marble. Seventeenth century. Italian.

Decoration

Black marble basin, lipped and mounted on a square marble pillar moulded where it joins the base. The splayed support between basin and pillar is carved with a leaf pattern.

The basin is surmounted by a pedimental feature containing a recessed carved face similar to a Pompeain fountain where water spouts from the mouth.

O.S. Ref. No. 493 993

ST. MICHAEL THORPE-LE-SOKEN

Church Foundation: The body of the church was rebuilt in 1876 on a site which, it is believed, has had a church since the twelfth century. The tower is early sixteenth century.

Monopod. Octagonal bowl. Perpendicular, fifteenth century.

Decoration

The rim of the octagonal bowl has been damaged and repaired in several places. The bowl has square recessed panelled faces each having a shield surrounded by a pointed octfoil with the exception of the west face which is plain and suggests that the font was originally against a wall or pier. It is known that the font was moved from the west end of the church to its present position in 1876 when the galleries were taken down. The octfoil may represent 'regeneration'. The underside of the bowl is hollow-chamfered to a half-round moulding under which is a short octagonal pedestal.

The east, north, west and south faces of the pedestal each have a recessed round-lobed quatrefoil with a florette in the centre and in each spandrel. The north-east, north-west, south-west and south-east faces each have two recessed cinquefoil headed window form panels.

The whole is mounted on a square sub-base with priest's step.

Cover

The cover is octagonal with vertical sides having short buttresses containing niches at the angles. Each side has a pierced round-lobed quatrefoil. Rising from the buttresses is a boarded cone having eight ribs and having the alternate sides pierced with a small trefoil headed lancet window form. The cone rises to a foliated finial of four inward curving leaves. Modern.

O.S. Ref. No. 179 223

ST. MARY MAGDALENE — THORRINGTON

Church Foundation: Decorated.

Monopod. Octagonal bowl. Perpendicular, fifteenth century.

Decoration

The octagonal bowl has suffered damage which has defaced some of the carving.
East face: Large foliate.
North-east face: Shield charged with three nails (Cruxifixion symbols).
North face: Phoenix rising from the flames (Rebirth).
North-west face: Shield defaced.
West face: Large foliate.
South-west face: Shield charged with lantern, pillar and sword (Crucifixion symbols).
South face: Blank.
South-east face: Large foilate.
Each shield is surrounded with a variety of fruits.
The bowl is cracked either side of south face.
The underside of the bowl is deep and heavily moulded with a curious pattern on the lower side of the bowl which is probably meant to represent water. (See Tendring).
The pedestal is octagonal the east, north, west and south faces having recessed lancet window tracery with trefoiled heads. The remaining faces have plain heads with a buttress in the centre of each face extending from the base to the top of the pedestal.
The top of the octagonal base is hollow-chamfered with the east, north, west and south sides of the chamfer each having a recessed foliate.
Under the chamfer is a deep quirk to shallow vertical sides.
The whole stands on a polygonal sub-base with priest's step.

O.S. Ref. No. 099 197

ST. PETER THUNDERSLEY

Church Foundation: Norman.

Monopod. Octagonal Bowl. Perpendicular, late fourteenth century.

Decoration

The octagonal bowl is small and each face is decorated with a deeply recessed pointed-lobed quatrefoil having a foliate in the centre. Each foliate is different.
The rim of the bowl is chamfered and the underside deeply hollow-chamfered to the octagonal pedestal and separated by a half-round moulding.
The base is hollow-chamfered at the top with a deep quirk under to a small two-stepped straight sided base.
The whole is mounted on a rectangular sub-base.

Cover

The cover is a flat octagonal wooden lid. Modern.

O.S. Ref. No. 783 886

ST. NICHOLAS TILLINGHAM

Church Foundation: Norman.

Polypod. Square bowl. Norman, late.

Decoration

On each of the four faces is carved a water-leaf design with the leaves bending from the centre of each face over to the corners. The support is massive being composed of a quatrefoil shaped pedestal with attached angle shafts used purely for decorative purposes. The shafts have plain rounded capitals with roll moulding and the reverse at the base. The whole stands on a large square base which in turn stands on a much larger sub-base with chamfered top edges together with priest's step.

O.S. Ref. No. 038 993

ST. MARY　　　　TOLLESBURY

Church Foundation: Early Norman.

Monopod. Octagonal bowl. Eighteenth century, c1718.

Decoration

The octagonal bowl is small with a hollow chamfer on the top edge. The faces are straight but the underside of the bowl is deeply chamfered to the stem.
The stem is octagonal with a deep octagonal base with moulding between stem and base.
Around the bowl are carved the words 'Good people all I pray take care, That in ye church you doe not sware. As this man did'.
It would appear that the font was obtained by a churchwarden named Robert Joyce in 1718 from a certain John Norman who came into the church talking and cursing during the service. In order that he would not be prosecuted Norman paid five pounds out of which this font was purchased.
Robert Joyce then had the above words carved round the bowl.

O.S. Ref. No. 957 104

ST. NICHOLAS　　　　TOLLESHUNT D'ARCY

Church Foundation: Early Perpendicular (built on site of earlier church).

Monopod. Octagonal bowl. Perpendicular, late fifteenth century.

Decoration

The bowl is octagonal with moulded rim and faces dividied by vertical ribs.
East face: Large rosette (seven petals) within cusped circle.
North-east face: Large uncharged shield.
North face: Large rosette (seven petals) within cusped circle.
North-west face: Large uncharged shield.
West face: Large rosette (seven petals) within cusped circle.
South-west face: Large shield charged with Latin cross the crossing arm of which has been chiselled away.
South face: Large rosette (seven petals) within cusped circle.
South-east face: Large uncharged shield.
Base of bowl is moulded on edge and chamfered to stem.
The large octagonal stem has buttresses, each with two set-offs, between alternate faces. The octagonal base has a hollow chamfered top edge. On the rim of the bowl it is possible to discern where the cover fastenings have been removed and the holes filled in. This is shown by two opposite lumps under the lead lining which apparently was inserted after the fastenings were removed.

O.S. Ref. No. 928 117

Church Foundation: Decorated.

Monopod. Half-octagonal bowl, placed against south wall.
Perpendicular, fifteenth century.

Decoration

The bowl is placed against the south wall and shows only five faces.
East face: Two shallow window forms with trefoiled heads.
North-east face: Large rosette (five petals) carved in relief.
North face: Uncharged shield carved in relief.
North-west face: Large rosette (five petals) carved in relief.
West face: Two shallow window forms with trefoiled heads.
Underside of bowl chamfered to stem.
Stem plain octagonal on base having hallow chamfer on top edge and cut off against the wall.

Cover

Flat wooden circular cover with stepped circular knob in centre. Modern.

O.S. Ref. No. 909 112

ALL SAINTS ULTING

Church Foundation: Early English.

Polypod. Octagonal bowl, Purbeck marble. Early English, thirteenth century.

Decoration

The Purbeck marble small octagonal bowl has one shallow pointed blank arch on each face. The angles are slightly chamfered and the bowl has been repaired in places.

The bowl is supported on a modern mount composed of a central drum stem with eight short detached shafts on an octagonal base on top of a deep octagonal sub-base which was obviously made to raise the height of the font to avoid the priest having to bend over.

O.S. Ref. No. 801 088

ST. LAURENCE — UPMINSTER

Church Foundation: Early English.

Monopod. Octagonal bowl. Perpendicular, fifteenth century.

Decoration

Recessed round lobed quatrefoils within circles on each face, each quatrefoil containing a fleuron in the centre.
Bowl separated from stem by roll moulding.
Octagonal stem, each side containing a trefoiled head lancet.
Top edge of base is chamfered and moulded.
Note. This font was originally provided by the Abbot of Waltham for the chapel at Upminster Hall and was presented to the Church by Mr. Champion Branfill when the chapel was dismantled in 1777.

Cover

The cover has an octagonal lid with moulded edge surmounted with a tall tapering octagonal stem. From each of four sides is a panel having curved buttressed sides with cusps and a projecting fleur-de-lis at the top. Each side is pierced with Decorated style window tracery. The central stem terminates with a 'poupee' head finial. Modern.

O.S. Ref. No. 559 866

ALL SAINTS

VANGE

Church Foundation: Norman.

Polypod. Square bowl. Transitional, twelfth century.

Decoration

West, south and north sides of bowl are plain but the east side has zig-zag motif.
The top of the rim has foliage decoration in the corners.
There are remains of lid fastenings in the rim.
The bowl rests on a large circular drum pedestal and four circular plain detached corner shafts having moulded circular bases and mounted on a square base.
The whole is mounted on a large modern square sub-base, 19th century.
The font is well worn.

Cover

The cover is composed on a flat circular lid with four carved ornamental radiating trusses, their inner edges being attached to a centrepiece having a Latin cross finial. Modern.

O.S. Ref. No. 274 875

ALL SAINTS WAKES COLNE

Church Foundation: Norman

Polypod. Hexagonal bowl, Purbeck marble.
Transitional, late twelfth century.

Decoration

The hexagonal bowl has three blank shallow round-headed arches on each face and each angle is slightly chamfered.
The rim shows marks of lid fastenings.
The bowl is mounted on a tall drum pedestal with three detached round supporting shafts on a stepped hexagonal base. The whole was restored in 1930 by Isabel Godbee.
This font was presented by Rev. Thomas Henderson, Vicar of Messing, 1846.

Cover

The hexagonal cover is composed of a lid with moulded top edge and boarded shallow cone rising to a cross finial.

O.S. Ref. No. 895 284

HOLY CROSS AND ST. LAWRENCE

WALTHAM ABBEY

Church Foundation: Norman on site of Previous Saxon Abbey

Monopod. Octagonal bowl, Purbeck marble. Late Norman, twlefth century.

Decoration

The bowl was originally square with arcaded sides and was polypod. Later, perhaps in the thirteenth century, it was re-cut into an octagonal bowl with plain faces supported on a round central pedestal having water-holding moulding at the bottom and standing on a square base.
The bowl is cracked around its centre and is chamfered on its bottom edge.
The whole is mounted on a deep octagonal sub-base.

Cover

The cover is a flat wooden lid with chamfered edge and floriated wrought-iron equal armed cross. Between the arms of the cross are four ring handles. Modern.

O.S. Ref. No. 381 007

ST. ANDREW WEELEY

Church Foundation: Rebuilt in 1881 with exception of 16c tower. Previous church was probably of early Norman foundation.

Monopod. Octagonal bowl. Perpendicular, latter part of fifteenth century.

Decoration

The rim of the octagonal bowl has been damaged where lid fastenings have been removed but since repaired.
The faces of the bowl are panelled and deeply recessed.
East, north, west and south faces each have round-lobed quatrefoil within a circle with square foliate in centre.
North-east, north-west, south-west and south-east faces each have a round-lobed quatrefoil within a circle with an uncharged shield in centre.
The underside of the bowl is moulded and chamfered with square foliate on each face of the chamfer.

The octagonal pedestal has identical cusped window tracery on each face.
The base is composed of a half-round moulding on top of a wide stepped chamfer with a deep quirk under which the vertical sides have chamfered top edges.
The whole is mounted on a modern rectangular sub-base with two chamfered corners and comprising a priest's step.

Cover

The cover is a flat wooden lid with crossed battens and wrought iron half-loop handle fastened to wrought iron cross pieces. Modern.

O.S. Ref. No. 145 223

ST. MARY THE VIRGIN　WENDENS AMBO

Church Foundation: Norman.

Monopod. Octagonal bowl. Decorated, fourteenth century.

Decoration

The bowl is a plain octagon. The top part is not part of the original font as it does not fit the lower portion. It may possibly be a restoration or replacement. The lower part of the bowl, pedestal and base would seem to be fourteenth century, but could be later.

The squat pedestal is octagonal and stands on a massive square base having a chamfered top edge with cut-off corners.

The font is attached to the westermost pier of the south arcade.

Cover

Sixteenth century.

The wooden boarded cover is domed and circular having curved plain ribs terminating with a wooden ball finial.

The cover is raised by a rope passing over a pulley housed in a wooden bracket projecting from the soffit of the arch.

O.S. Ref. No. 513 364

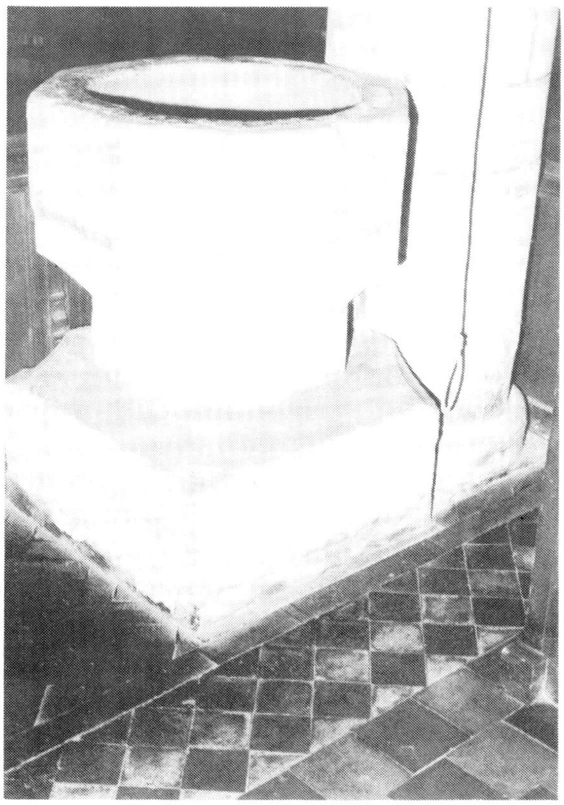

ST. MARY AND ST. PETER — WENNINGTON

Church Foundation: Norman.

Monopod. Octagonal bowl, Purbeck marble. Early English, thirteenth century.

Decoration

The octagonal bowl is plain and has been badly damaged. The rim has been completely covered in lead being a continuation of the bowl lining.
The short pedestal is plain and octagonal as is the base which is deep compared with the pedestal. The top edge is chamfered and damaged. The font has been subjected to various coats of paint which has obscured the original surface.

Cover

The plain font has an attractively carved oak cover which is Jacobean (seventeenth century). It is a shallow octagonal drum with strapwork cresting on the top of each side. Four ogee trusses support a central square baluster which terminates in an urn finial.

O.S. Ref. No. 539 809

ST. MARY — WEST BERGHOLT

Church Foundation: Saxo-Norman, eleventh century, overlaying an earlier timber church.

Monopod. Circular bowl. Early English, thirteenth century.

Decoration

The circular bowl is entirely plain and the rim has been damaged where lid fastenings have been removed. Part of the bowl on the west side has been cut out. Was it originally against a wall or pillar?

The large square pedestal has stop-chamfered angles and is mounted on a large square tiled base with stone surround. There is graffiti on the sides of the pedestal but both the bowl and pedestal have been whitewashed.

Cover

The cover is a flat plain wooden lid with chamfered edge and acorn finial. Date unknown.

O.S. Ref. No. 954 281

ST. MARY AND ST. EDWARD WEST HANNINGFIELD

Church Foundation: Norman.

Monopod. Octagonal bowl. Decorated, early fourteenth century.

Decoration

The bowl has tendril carving around the top under which is a deeply cut quirk. It would seem that the bowl has at some time been cut down and the moulded stone between the bowl and pedestal is of later date.

The base of the bowl is decorated with ball-flowers and quaint heads.

The stem is octagonal and is decorated on each face with trellis carving containing fleurons.

The whole is mounted on a base of Purbeck marble which once supported an older font of c1200.

Cover

The oak cover is composed of an octagonal lid moulded on the edge with radiating trusses to form a crown. The eight trusses rise from the angles meeting at the head of a central turned post just below a bulbous spiked finial.

O.S. Ref. No. 735 998

ST. PETER AND ST. PAUL WEST MERSEA

Church Foundation: Early Norman.

Monopod. Octagonal bowl, Purbeck marble. Early English, thirteenth century.

Decoration

Each face of the bowl has two blank shallow pointed arches. The bowl, which has been damaged and repaired, is mounted on a drum pedestal which may have come from near by Roman ruins. The pedestal rests on a three-stepped brick base mounted on a stone sub-base with chamfered top edge.

O.S. Ref. No. 009 125

ST. MARY MAGDALENE — WETHERSFIELD

Church Foundation: Transitional c1200 (probably built on site of Anglo-Norman church).

Monopod. Hexagonal. Perpendicular, fifteenth century.

Decoration

The hexagonal bowl has plain uncarved faces and the base of the bowl is lipped and moulded.

The pedestal is hexagonal with trefoil-headed window forms on each side separated by niched buttresses each culminating with an offset. The base is moulded.

This old font was moved to the south porch in the nineteenth century when a copy was placed in the church.

The copy is similar except that it has decorated faces.

East face: A shield charged with a form of quadrate cross within an octfoil. On each side is a trefoil-headed lancet window form.

North-east face: A shield charged with the letters IHC (Jesus) within an octfoil. On each side is a trefoil-headed lancet window form.

North-west face: A shield charged with a form of quadrate cross within an octfoil. On each side is a trefoil-headed lancet window form.

West face: A shield charged with the letters IHC within an octfoil. On each side is a trefoil-headed lancet window form.

South-east face: A shield charged with a monogram comprising the letters MSV within an octfoil. On each side is a trefoil-headed lancet window form.

Cover

The wooden cover is cone-shaped and boarded with concave moulded ribs rising to a finial. On the east side is a raised Latin cross.

O.S. Ref. No. 712 313

ST. ETHELDREDA
(Original Dedication Lost)

WHITE NOTLEY

Church Foundation: Early Norman built on site of previous Saxon church.

Monopod. Octagonal bowl. Perpendicular, c1400.

Decoration

The rim is hollow chamfered and the carving on each face is deeply recessed. The corners of the bowl have been repaired with iron strips which have rusted causing further damage. Evidence of damage caused by removal of cover fastenings.

East face: Round-headed quatrefoil within a circle with head in centre.

North-east face: Round-headed quatrefoil within a circle with a foliate in centre.

North face: Round-headed quatrefoil within a circle with uncharged shield in centre.

North-west face: Round-headed quatrefoil within a circle with a figure which perhaps represents a baby wearing a chrisom robe.

West face: Round-headed quatrefoil within a circle with a shield in centre.

South-west face: Round-headed quatrefoil within a circle with a foliate in centre.

South face: Round-headed quatrefoil within a circle with a rosette in centre.

South-east face: Round-headed quatrefoil within a circle with a shield in centre.

The underside of bowl is moulded and chamfered to stem with rosettes on each face.

The octagonal stem has various traceried window forms deeply recessed on the faces.

The base is stepped, each step being chamfered the whole being mounted on a rectangular stone which includes a priest's step.

Cover

The flat wooden lid has an equal armed wrought iron cross with fleur-de-lis ends and twisted ring handle in centre.

O.S. Ref. No. 785 182

ST. MARTIN — WHITE RODING

Church Foundation: Norman.

Monopod. Square bowl, Purbeck marble. Norman, twelfth century.

Decoration

Incised zig-zag decoration on each face.
Incised concentric circles in spandrels on rim top.
The bowl sits on a drum pedestal and square base with chamfered top edge made up of different types of stone of later date.
The whole is mounted on a rectangular sub-base with priest's step which contains moulds for taper making.

O.S. Ref. No. 562 134

ST. MARGARET WICKEN BONHUNT

Church Foundation: Early English (Disused Norman chapel of St. Helens nearby).

Polypod. Square bowl. Norman, c1200.

Decoration

The square rough hewn bowl is plain and has marks of lid fastenings on the rim. The bowl is mounted on a central shaft and four corner shafts having square capitals and bases with stop chamfers on the shafts' angles.
The whole is mounted on a square base with priest's step having a wooden surround which in turn is mounted on a large tiled sub-base.

Cover

The cover is a round flat wooden lid with chamfered edge. The ironwork consists of an equal-armed cross with fleur-de-lis ends, a central circle with a semi-circle and fleur-de-lis within the angles of the cross. In the centre is a cable ring handle. Modern.

O.S. Ref. No. 499 334

ST. CATHERINE (Original dedication unknown) — WICKFORD

Church Foundation: Rebuilt 1876 using some materials from old church.

Monopod. Octagonal bowl. Perpendicular, fifteenth century.

Decoration

The octagonal bowl has plain faces and the underside is slightly hollow-chamfered to a half-round moulding.
The pedestal is octagonal and plain with half-round mouldings at top and bottom.
The base is octagonal and hollow-chamfered to short vertical sides.
The whole is mounted on a rectangular sub-base with chamfered corners on north side.

Cover

The cover is a flat octagonal wooden lid with moulded edge. In the centre are four brass arms each ending with a fleur-de-lis and having a central stem with four concave supports rising to a patée cross finial. Modern.

O.S. Ref. No. 745 933.

ST. CHRISTOPHER WILLINGALE DOE

Church Foundation: Norman.

Monopod. Octagonal bowl. Perpendicular, fifteenth century.

Decoration

The large octagonal bowl is damaged on the rim probably where staples have been wrenched out.
Each face has a recessed round-lobed quatrefoil within a circle with uncharged shield in centre. Some of the shields contain graffiti. The underside of the bowl is moulded and hollow-chamfered with half-round moulding to pedestal.
The octagonal pedestal has a trefoil-headed lancet window form on each face and is mounted on a small octagonal base having chamfered top edge.

Cover

The cover is a circular wooden lid decorated with a recessed wooden cross having arms radiating from a wooden circular disc in centre on which is a short baluster handle with ball finial. Modern.

O.S. Ref. No. 594 076

ST. ANDREW WILLINGALE SPAIN

Church Foundation: Norman.

Monopod. Octagonal bowl. Perpendicular, fifteenth century.

Decoration

East, north-west and south faces each have a recessed head in a round-lobed quatrefoil within a circle. The north face head appears to be encircled with rays of glory.
North-east, north-west, south-west and south-east faces each have a recessed foliate or rosette in a round-lobed quatrefoil within a circle.
The underside of the small bowl is moulded and foliated.
The stem is octagonal with a cinque-foiled lancet window form on each face with a recessed round-lobed quatrefoil under.
The octagonal base has a chamfered top edge with a fleuron on the chamfer on each side. Below is a recessed round-lobed quatrefoil flanked by a cinque-foiled lancet window form on each side and finished with moulding under. The whole rests on an octagonal sub-base.

O.S. Ref. No. 596 073

ST. MARY-THE-VIRGIN WIVENHOE

Church Foundation: Early perpendicular.

Monopod. Octagonal bowl. Perpendicular, c.1500.

Decoration

East face: Round-lobed quatrefoil containing fleurette.
North-east face: Uncharged shield in octfoil.
North face: Fleurette in round-lobed quatrefoil within circle.
North-west face: Uncharged shield in octfoil.
West face: Blank.
South-west face: Uncharged shield in octfoil.
South face: Fleurette in round-lobed quatrefoil within circle.
South-east face: Uncharged shield in octfoil.
Underside of bowl chamfered to pedestal.
Octagonal pedestal with plain faces with octagonal base chamfered on top edge and mounted on a sub-base.

O.S. Ref. No. 039 215

ST. MARY-THE-VIRGIN WOODHAM FERRERS

Church Foundation: Late early English.

Monopod. Octagonal bowl, damaged. Decorated, c1300.

Decoration

The faces of the octagonal bowl are plain and the underside is deeply moulded and hollow-chamfered to the short pedestal.
The pedestal is plain, octagonal and the base is composed of a long hollow-chamfer to short straight sides.
The whole is mounted on a small octagonal sub-base with priest's step.

Cover

The cover is composed of a shallow enclosed lid from which rise eight thin open ogee trusses terminating in an octagonal pointed finial. Modern.

O.S. Ref. No. 797 994

ST. MICHAEL THE ARCHANGEL — WOODHAM WALTER

Church Foundation: Elizabethan, sixteenth century (1563).

Monopod. Octagonal bowl, Clunch. Perpendicular, late fourteenth or early fifteenth century. There seems to be little doubt that this font came from the previous church the site of which has not been definitely established.

Decoration

The east, north, west and south faces each has two trefoiled head lancets.
The north-east, north-west, south-west and south-east faces each has an uncharged shield in a round-lobed quatrefoil within a circle.
The rim has been damaged by the wrenching out of the hasp and staple. Part of the staple still remains.
The pedestal is octagonal with a trefoiled head lancet on each face.
The underside of the bowl is chamfered to the pedestal each face of the chamfer containing an undecorated square. The chamfer is finished with a half-round moulding.
The pedestal stands on an octagonal moulded base with priest's step. Modern. At some time the step has been higher than at present and this has left scars on the base of the pedestal.

Cover

Circa 1700.
The cover is octagonal with a moulded base. Short inset straight faces rise to battlemented tops from which rises a solid pyramidal top like a parapet spire terminating with a carved finial.
On the base are carved the words 'Suffer little children to come unto me' and the short straight faces are decorated with:
East face: Ark.
North face: Dove of Peace.
West face: Cross.
South face: Crown.
The cover is raised by a pulley mechanism having an ornamented iron weight.

O.S. Ref. No. 858 068

ALL SAINTS WRABNESS

Church Foundation: Norman.

Monopod. Octagonal bowl. Perpendicular, fifteenth century.

Decoration

The whole of the octagonal font has suffered severe damage and deliberate defacement and the bowl is cracked.
The rim contains remains of lid fastenings.
The faces were originally recessed carved panels of the Evangelists and their symbols but have been so defaced that no recognition is possible.
The underside of the bowl has a winged angel at each angle with a fleurette in between each angel but once again much defaced.
The pedestal has remains of four buttresses and in between are the remains of four figures.
The base is square with chamfered top edge and corners and does not appear to be part of original font.
The whole is supported by an iron cage support on a rectangular sub-base with chamfered corners incorporating a priest's step which are modern.

Cover

The cover is a plain flat octagonal wooden lid with chamfered edge decorated with small incised triangles.

O.S. Ref. No. 174 319

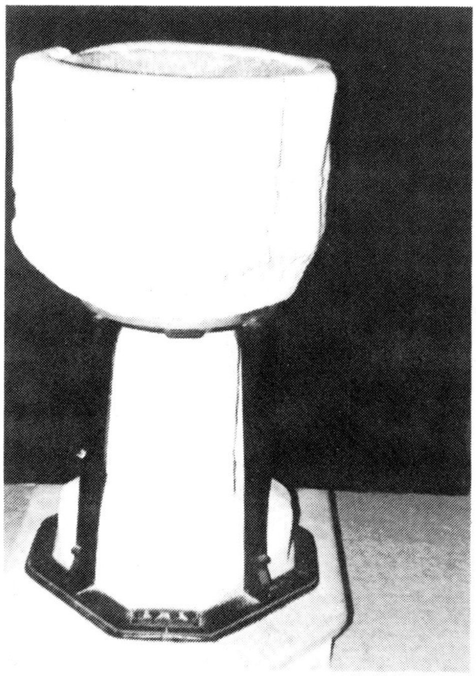

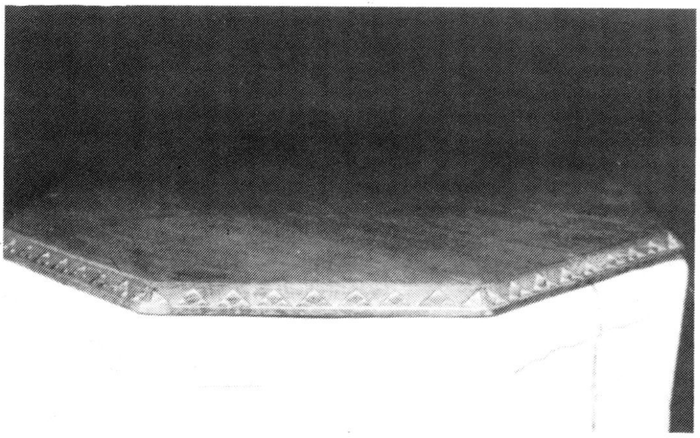

Church Foundation: Early English.

Mounted on low base. Square bowl of rough Caen stone. Norman, c1170.

Decoration

Square bowl has plain sides with attached corner shafts having scalloped capitals and moulded bases.
The bowl is now mounted on a low moulded base (1869), but was originally mounted on four shafts at the angles.
North-east corner of rim of bowl is broken away where removal of the staple has been attempted but which is still in situ.
This font is very similar to the one in Norton Mandeville church.

O.S. Ref. No. 678 062

Addendum (details not included in indices)

ST. ANDREW ABBERTON

Church Foundation: Fourteenth century.

Monopod. Octagonal bowl. Fifteenth century, perpendicular.

Decoration

The octagonal bowl had plain rough finished faces. The rim is much damaged where the lid fastenings have been removed.
Underneath, the base of the bowl is rounded to meet the plain octagonal pedestal. The octagonal base begins by being slightly proud of the pedestal then opening out with a hollow chamfer to shallow sides.
The font has at some time in the past been painted and remains of this may still be seen.

Cover – Modern

The octagonal wooden cover is made up of three flat octagonal boards decreasing in size and each moulded on the edges. In the centre rises an octagonal ogee shaped centre piece terminating in a floriate finial. On one side are the carved words 'A thank offering for Victory 1939-1945'.

O.S. Ref. No. 997 194

Addendum (details not included in indices)

ST. MARY THE VIRGIN EASTHORPE

Church Foundation: Norman.

Polypod. Octagonal bowl. Thirteenth century, Early English.

Decoration

The bowl of this font would appear to be Early English but it is surprising that there are no indications of their having been any lid fastenings. There is no reason, however, to suggest the authenticity of the bowl.

At the base of each face of the bowl there is a rounded trefoil-headed three ordered arch, each arch being supported on a round shaft having Early English moulded capitals and bases. The central pedestal is octagonal having concave sides with shafts at the angles. The whole rests on a shallow octagonal base which with the pedestal and shafts are Victorian.

O.S. Ref. No. 913 215

CHURCH DEDICATIONS

All Saints
Ashdon
Barling
Brightlingsea
Creeksea
Doddinghurst
Dovercourt
Epping Upland
Great Horkesley
Great Oakley
High Laver
High Roding
Little Totham
Nazeing
North Benfleet
Norton Mandeville
Rayne
Rickling
Springfield
Stock
Sutton
Terling
Ulting
Vange
Wakes Colne
Wrabness
Writtle

All Saints and St. Faiths
Childerditch

Annunciation of the Blessed Virgin Mary
Prittlewell

Holy Cross
Felsted

Holy Cross and St. Lawrence
Waltham Abbey

Holy Trinity
Bradwell-juxta-Coggeshall
Chrishall
Colchester
Littlebury
North Fambridge
Takeley

St. Albright
Stanway

St. Andrew
Althorne
Ashingdon
Belchamp St. Paul
Boreham
Bulmer
Fingringhoe
Halstead
Helion Bumpstead
Heybridge
Marks Tey
Sandon
Shalford
Weeley
Willingale Spain

St. Augustine of Canterbury
Ashen
Birdbrook

St. Barnabas
Alphamstone
Great Tey

St. Botolph
Hadstock

St. Catherine
East Tilbury
Wickford

St. Christopher
Willingale Doe

St. Edmund
Abbess Roding

St. Edmund King and Martyr
East Mersea
Tendring

St. Etheldreda
White Notley

St. George
Pentlow

St. Germans
Bobbingworth
Faulkbourne

St. Giles
Great Maplestead
Langford
Mountnessing

St. Giles and All Saints
Orsett

St. Helen and St. Giles
Rainham

St. James
Little Clacton

St. James-the-Great
Great Sailing

St. James-the-Less
Hadleigh

St. John
Finchingfield

St. John-the-Baptist
Great Clacton
Little Maplestead
Little Yeldham
Thaxted

St. John-the-Evangelist
Havering-atte-Bower
Langley
Little Leighs

St. Lawrence or St. Laurence
Blackmore
Bradfield
Steeple
Upminster

St. Laurence and All Saints
Eastwood

St. Leonard
Southminster
The Hythe, Colchester

St. Margaret
Bowers Gifford
Margaret Roding
Margaretting
Stanford Rivers
Wicken Bonhunt

St. Margaret-of-Antioch
Stanford le Hope

St. Martin
White Roding

CHURCH DEDICATIONS *(Continued)*

St. Martin-of-Tours
Chipping Ongar

St. Mary
Belchamp Walter
Birchanger
Broomfield
Burnham-on-Crouch
Chickney
Elsenham
Fryerning
Great Dunmow
Great Leighs
Great Parndon
Lawford
Little Burstead
Little Dunmow
Ramsden Bellhouse
Runwell
Stapleford Tawney
Stifford
Strethall
Tollesbury
West Bergholt

St. Mary and all Saints
Great Stambridge
Lambourne End
Rivenhall

St. Mary and St. Clement
Clavering

St. Mary and St. Edward
West Hanningfield

St. Mary and St. Lawrence
Great Waltham

St. Mary Magdalene
Billericay
Great Burstead
Thorrington
Wethersfield

St. Mary and St. Margaret
Stow Maries

St. Mary and St. Peter
Wennington

St. Mary-the-Virgin
Arkesden
Copford
Corringham
Dedham
Gestingthorpe
Great Bentley
Henham
High Easter
Lindsell
Little Baddow
Little Bentley
Little Bromley
Little Chesterford
Little Laver
Little Wakering
Maldon
Matching
Moreton
Newport
North Shoebury
Ovington
Peldon
Saffron Walden
Sheering
Shenfield
Stansted Mountfitchet
Stebbing
Steeple Bumpstead
Wendens Ambo
Wivenhoe
Woodham Ferrers

St. Mary-the-Virgin and all Saints
Debden

St. Mary and St. Edward
West Hanningfield

St. Michael
Aveley
Fobbing
Great Sampford
Thorpe-le-Soken

St. Michael and all Angels
Leaden Roding

St. Michael-the-Archangel
Theydon Mount
Woodham Walter

St. Nicholas
Canewdon
Chignal Smealey
Fyfield
Great Wakering
Harwich
Ingrave
Kelvedon Hatch
Laindon
Tillingham
Tolleshunt D'Arcy
Tolleshunt Major

St. Peter
Little Warley
Roydon
South Weald
Thundersley

St. Peter-Ad-Vincula
Great Coggeshall

St. Peter and St. Paul
Bardfield Saling
Black Notley
Chingford
Grays
Hockley
Horndon-on-the-Hill
St. Osyth
Stondon Massey
West Mersea

St. Peter and St. Thomas
Stambourne

St. Stephen
Great Wigborough

St. Thomas-the-Apostle
Bradwell-juxta-Mare

LOCATION OF FONTS OF VARIOUS PERIODS

Norman
Abbess Roding
Alphamstone
Arkesden
Aveley
Belchamp Walter
Bradwell-juxta-Coggeshall
Burnham-on-Crouch
Eastwood
Fryerning
Great Oakley
Hadstock
Havering-atte-Bower
Little Laver
Little Maplestead
Little Wakering
Norton Mandeville
Ovington
Peldon
Pentlow
Rainham
Sheering
Tillingham
Waltham Abbey
White Roding
Wicken Bonhunt
Writtle

Early English (including Transitional)
Ashdon
Blackmore
Bradfield
Broomfield
Canewdon
Chingford
Clavering
Copford
Corringham
Epping Upland
Felsted
Fobbing
Fyfield
Great Coggeshall
Great Wakering
Great Waltham
Hadleigh
Harwich
Hockly
Laindon
Littlebury
Little Chesterford
Little Clacton
Little Leighs
Moreton
Newport
North Benfleet
North Shoebury
Springfield
Stanford-le-Hope
Stanford Rivers
Stansted Mountfitchet
Stifford Strethall
Sutton
Terling
Ulting
Vange
Wakes Colne
Wennington
West Bergholt
West Mersea

Decorated
Ashen
Black Notley
Boreham
Bradwell-juxta-Mare
Chipping Ongar
Chrishall
Dedham
Doddinghurst
Finchingfield
Great Dunmow
Great Sampford
Horndon-on-the-Hill
Leaden Roding
Little Dunmow
Rayne
Rivenhall
Roydon
Sandon
Stebbing
Wendens Ambo
West Hanningfield
Woodham Ferrers

Perpendicular (Including Early Tudor)
Althorne
Ashingdon
Bardfield Saling
Barling
Belchamp St. Paul
Birchanger
Black Notley
Bobbingworth
Bowers Gifford
Brightlingsea
Bulmer
Chickney
Chignal Smealey
Childerditch
Colchester
Creeksea
Dovercourt
East Mersea
East Tilbury
Faulkbourne
Fingringhoe
Gestingthorpe
Grays
Great Bentley
Great Burstead
Great Clacton
Great Leighs
Great Maplestead
Great Parndon
Great Saling
Great Stambridge
Great Tey
Great Wigborough
Halstead
Helion Bumpstead
Henham
High Easter
High Laver
High Roding
Ingrave
Kelvedon Hatch
Langford
Langley
Lindsell

Perpendicular *(continued)*
Liston
Little Bentley
Little Bromley
Little Burstead
Little Totham
Little Yeldham
Margaret Roding
Margaretting
Marks Tey
Matching
Mountnessing
Nazeing
North Fambridge
Orsett
Prittlewell
Ramsdem Bellhouse
Rickling
Runwell
Saffron Walden
Shalford
Shenfield
Southminster
Stambourne
Stanway
Steeple
Steeple Bumpstead
Stock
Stonden Massey
Stow Maries
Thaxted
The Hythe, Colchester
Thorpe-le-Soken
Thorrington
Thundersley
Tolleshunt D'Arcy
Tolleshunt Major
Upminster
Weeley
Wethersfield
White Notley
Wickford
Willingale Doe
Willingale Spain
Wivenhoe
Woodham Walter
Wrabness

Post-Reformation to Eighteenth Century (Including Late Tudor)
Billericay
Birdbrook
Debden
Elsenham
Lambourne End
Lawford
Little Warley
Maldon
Rayne
St. Osyth
South Weald
Stapleford Tawney
Tendring
Theydon Mount
Tollesbury

NUMBERS OF FONTS OF VARIOUS SHAPES AND NUMBERS OF MONOPOD AND POLYPOD FONTS

Norman

Square	17	
Octagonal	4	
Circular	5	26
Monopod	13	
Polypod	11	
Classed as unmounted	2	

Early English (including transitional)

Square	17	
Octagonal	19	
Circular	3	
Octfoil	1	
Hexagonal	1	41
Monopod	11	
Polypod	30	

Decorated

Square	3	
Octagonal	18	
Hexagonal	1	22
Monopod	19	
Polypod	2	
Classed as unmounted	1	

Perpendicular

Octagonal	87	
Hexagonal	2	89
Monopod	86	
Polypod	3	

Post-Reformation

Square	1	
Round	3	
Rectangular	1	
Octagonal	10	
Hexagonal	1	16
Monopod	16	

GLOSSARY

Acanthus: Form of ornament based on the broad scalloped leaf of the acanthus plant.
Affusion: Pouring of water over the head.
Agnes Dei: 'The Lamb of God' referring to Christ in His sacrificial role.
Annulet: Ring round a shaft.
Aspersion: Sprinkling.
Ball Flower: An ornament of globular shape resembling a three-petalled flower enclosing a small ball.
Baluster: A small pillar or column used as a support.
Baptistry: A building for baptismal rites containing the font, often separate from the church.
Bifurcated: Divide into two branches.
Billet: A moulding consisting of short cylindrical or rectangular blocks or billets placed at regular intervals in a hollow moulding.
Blank Arcading: A succession of arches enriching a wall or other face but unpierced and used as decoration.
Botonée Cross: Having round-headed trefoiled ends.
Broach Spire: An octagonal spire on a square tower. Each of the four vacant spaces at the joining of octagon and square is filled by a half pyramid which is the broach.
Buttress: A mass of masonry or brickwork built against a wall to give it stability.
Cable Ornament: Resembling a cable or rope.
Canon: A rule set by the Church.
Catchumen: Candidate ready for baptism.
Chalice: Cup or vessel used for wine at Mass or Communion service.
Chamfer: The surface formed when a square angle is cut away obliquely.
Chantry: Name given to a chapel or altar or any part of a church where priests chanted prayers on behalf of the dead or for the particular founder.
Cherub: Member of one of the Angelic Orders usually depicted as a child's head with wings.
Chevron: Moulding forming a zig zag.
Chrism: Consecrated oil.
Chrisom: White cloth laid on child at baptism.
Cinquefoil: Having five foils.
Clunch: A soft white limestone – a hard chalk.
Colonette: A diminutive column.
Concave: Curving inwards.
Cone: Figure with curved base tapering to a point.
Convex: Curving outwards.
Corbel: Projecting block supporting a beam or horizontal member.
Coronal: Circlet.
Counterpoise: Weight which balances another weight.
Crocket: Carved projection usually of stylised leaf form.
Cushion Capital: Cut from cube having lower part rounded off.
Cusp: Point separating foliations (see Foliated).
Dagger Counterfoil: Dagger shaped.
Diapering: Repetitive geometrical decoration.
Exorcism: The driving out through words and actions evil or diabolic power.
Fillet: Narrow band used to separate two mouldings or to terminate a series of mouldings.
Fimbriated: Fringed.
Finial: An ornament crowning a pinnacle or any other form.
Fleur-de-Lis (Lys): French for lily flower.
Fleurée: An equal-armed cross having a floriated trefoil at end of each arm.
Fleurette or Fleuron: Decorative carved flower or leaf
Floriated: Decorated with floral ornament.
Fluting: Shallow concave grooves running vertically.
Flying Buttress: An arch used to carry the thrust of a vault or roof from walls of a building to an outer pier or buttress.
Foil: Each of the small arc openings in Gothic tracery separated by cusps e.g. trefoil (3), quatrefoil (4), cinquefoil (5), multifoil (many).
Foliated: Any surface covered with leaf ornament.
Font: A vessel to contain the water used in baptism. Usually placed near the west end of a church.
Freestone: Fine grained building stone capable of being worked in any direction.
Fresco: Painting with water-colour on walls while plaster was still wet.
Gable: Head of wall at end of a double-pitched roof.
Gadrooning: Ornamental border of repeating convex ribs.
Gothic: The style of architecture comprising the periods known as Early English, Decorated and Perpendicular.
Graffiti: Drawings or markings scratched on walls and other places.
Greek Cross: Plain equal armed cross.
Guild: A fraternity formed to protect the interests of workmen of different crafts. The religious fraternities were devoted to the well-being of church members.
Hemi-Spherical: Half of a sphere.
Hexagonal: Six sided.
Hollow Chamfer: Chamfer with concave surface. (See chamfer).
Immersion: Baptism by plunging under water.
Incised: Cut into – engraved.
Intersecting Arcading: A succession of round-headed arches intersecting one with the other and producing a series of pointed arches.
Jesse, Tree of: Tree with branches showing descent of Christ from Jesse through his son David.
Lancet: Shaped like narrow arch with pointed top.
Latin Cross: Plain cross having three equal length arms, the lower vertical arm being longer. Adapted from the equal armed Greek cross to take the transfixed body of Christ.
Linenhold: Pattern resembling linen arranged in vertical folds.
Lobe: Projection, rounded or pointed.
Lozenge: A diamond shape.
Misericord: A bracket on the underside of a hinged choir stall seat which when the seat is turned up gives support during long periods of standing.
Monopod: Tri-partite consisting of a bowl, central pedestal and base.
Moulding: A plain or enriched projection or recessed band.
Multifoil: See 'Foil'.
Necking: Narrow moulding round the bottom of a capital between it and the shaft of the column.
Niche: Small recess in a wall to contain a statue.
Octfoil: Having eight foils.
Ogee: A double curved line made up of a concave and a convex part similar to a letter S or inverted S.
Orb: Globe, maybe surmounted by a cross.
Passion Cross: A cross having pointed ends to the arms.
Patée Cross: A cross with the arms having a broad flat end.
Pedestal: The central support for a monopod font.

GLOSSARY *(Continued)*

Pediment: A low pitched triangular or segmental gable.
Pallet Moulding: Small rounded bosses.
Pendants: Elongated bosses projecting downwards or suspended.
Per Pale: Shield divided vertically up the middle.
Pinnacle: A small turret-like termination crowning spires, buttresses, parapets etc. Usually pyramid or conical shaped.
Piscina: A water drain in the floor or wall near an altar.
Polychrome: In many colours.
Polypod: Type of font having four or more legs as supports.
Pontificals: Book containing forms for rites performed by a Bishop.
Poupée Head: The raised and ornamental top of the ends of church benches often cut in the form of a fleur-de-lis.
Quadrate: Square.
Quatrefoil: See 'Foil'.
Quirk: An acute V-shaped groove.
Quoins: Dressed stones at the angles of a building.
Rituale Romanum: A book containing the rites and services of the Church of Rome.
Roll Moulding: A plain round moulding of semi-circular or more than semi-circular sections.
Romanesque: After the Roman style.
Saltire Cross: Figure formed by the diagonals of a rectangle.
Scalloped: A type of cushion capital in which the four sides are shaped into a series of curves or scallops. (truncated cones).
Scroll: An ornament in the form of a scroll of paper partly rolled.
Sedilia: A series of seats on the south side of the chancel for the use of clergy.
Seraph: Angel.
Set-offs: Projections against weather on the changing face of projections or buttresses.
Soffit: Underside of an arch.
Spandrel: Space between curve of arch and rectangle enclosing it.
Spur: Diagonal projection at base of a moulding or column.
Staple: U-shaped loop of metal driven into something to fasten something.
Stiff Leaf: A late twelfth century and early thirteenth century type of sculptored foliage.
Stop Chamfer: Ornamental termination to a chamfer.
String Course Moulding: Projecting horizontal band or moulding set in the surface of a wall.
Strapwork: Interlaced bands and forms similar to fretwork.
Synod: Ecclesiastical council.
Tabernacle: An elaborately carved canopy or cover suspended over a font.
Tendril: Slender thread-like carving.
Tracery: Ornamental intersecting work.
Transom: Horizontal member dividing a window.
Trefoil: See 'Foil'.
Triquetra: Ornamental formed of three interlacing almond shapes symbolising the Trinity.
Truss: A number of timbers framed together to bridge a space and to be self-supporting.
Uncharged Shield: A plain shield not painted or carved with a coat-of-arms.
Unction: Annointing with oil.
Vault: A roof constructed of stone.
Volute: Spiral scroll.
Water-Holding Moulding: Form of Gothic moulding having a round hollow capable of holding water.
Whorl: Single coil of a spiral.

BIBLIOGRAPHY

There are few books which deal with church fonts and font covers in any detail but the following list will be found useful.

F. D. Anderson — **History and Imagery in British Churches, 1971.**
Francis Bond — **Fonts and Font covers, 1908.**
J. Charles Cox and Alfred Harvey — **English Church Furniture, 1907**
J. G. Davies — **A Dictionary of Liturgy and Worship, 1972.**
Tyrrell-Green — **Baptismal Fonts, 1928.**
J. G. Davies — **The Architectural Setting of Baptism, 1962.**
Nikolaus Pevsner — **The Buildings of England – Essex.**
George Buckler — **Churches of Essex, 1856.**

INDEX – LOCATION OF ESSEX FONTS

INDEX — GENERAL

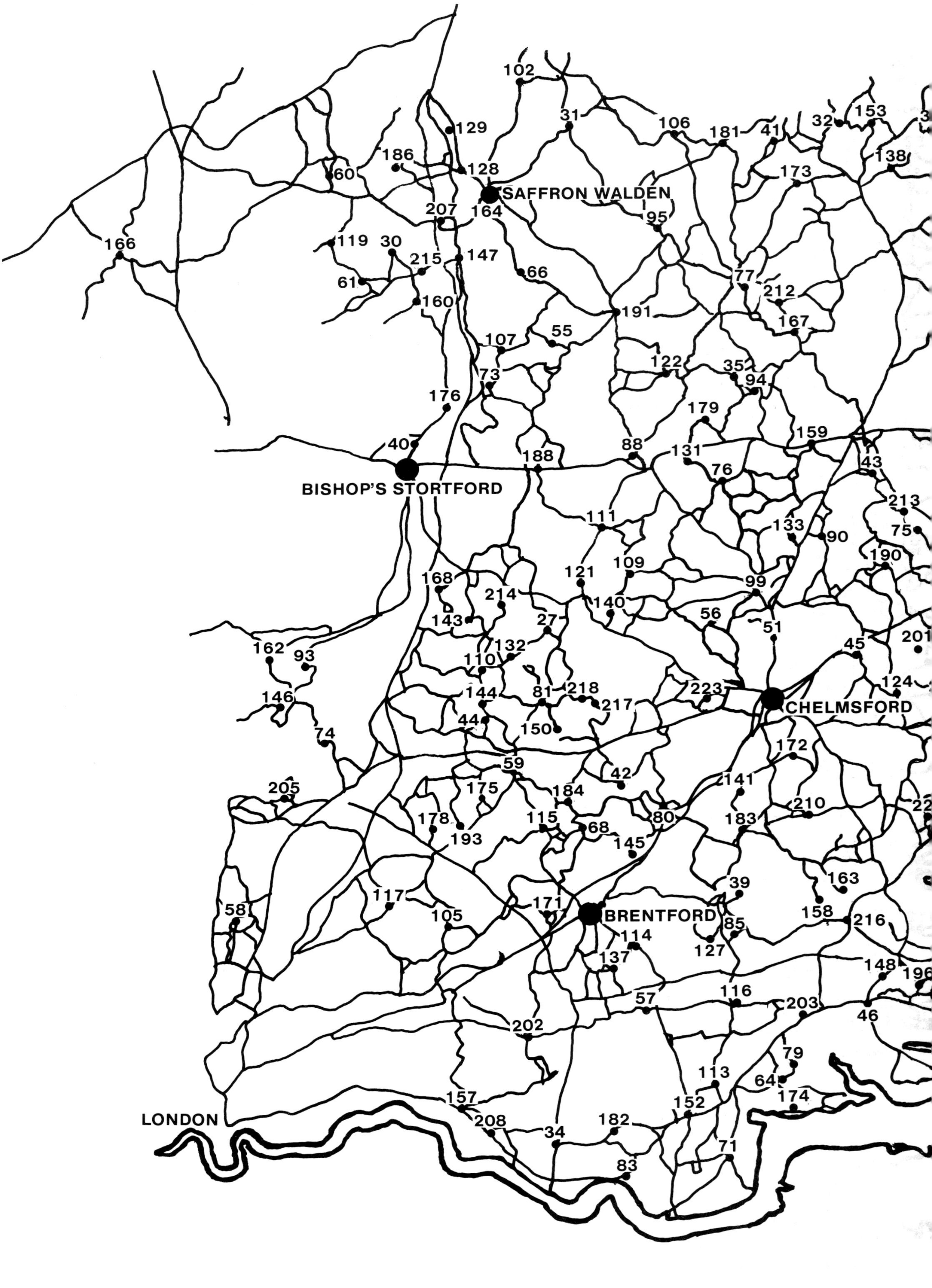

102
31
106
181
41
32
153
129
186
128
60
SAFFRON WALDEN
138
173
207
164
95
166
119
30
215
147
66
61
160
77
212
191
167
107
55
122
35
73
94
176
179
40
88
131
159
188
43
BISHOP'S STORTFORD
76
213
111
133
90
75
190
168
121
109
99
214
140
143
27
56
51
201
162
93
132
45
110
124
146
144
81
218
223
217
CHELMSFORD
44
150
74
59
172
42
141
205
175
184
210
178
115
68
80
183
193
145
163
39
117
171
58
105
BRENTFORD
158
216
85
114
127
137
148
196
57
116
203
46
202
79
113
64
157
174
152
LONDON
208
34
182
71
83

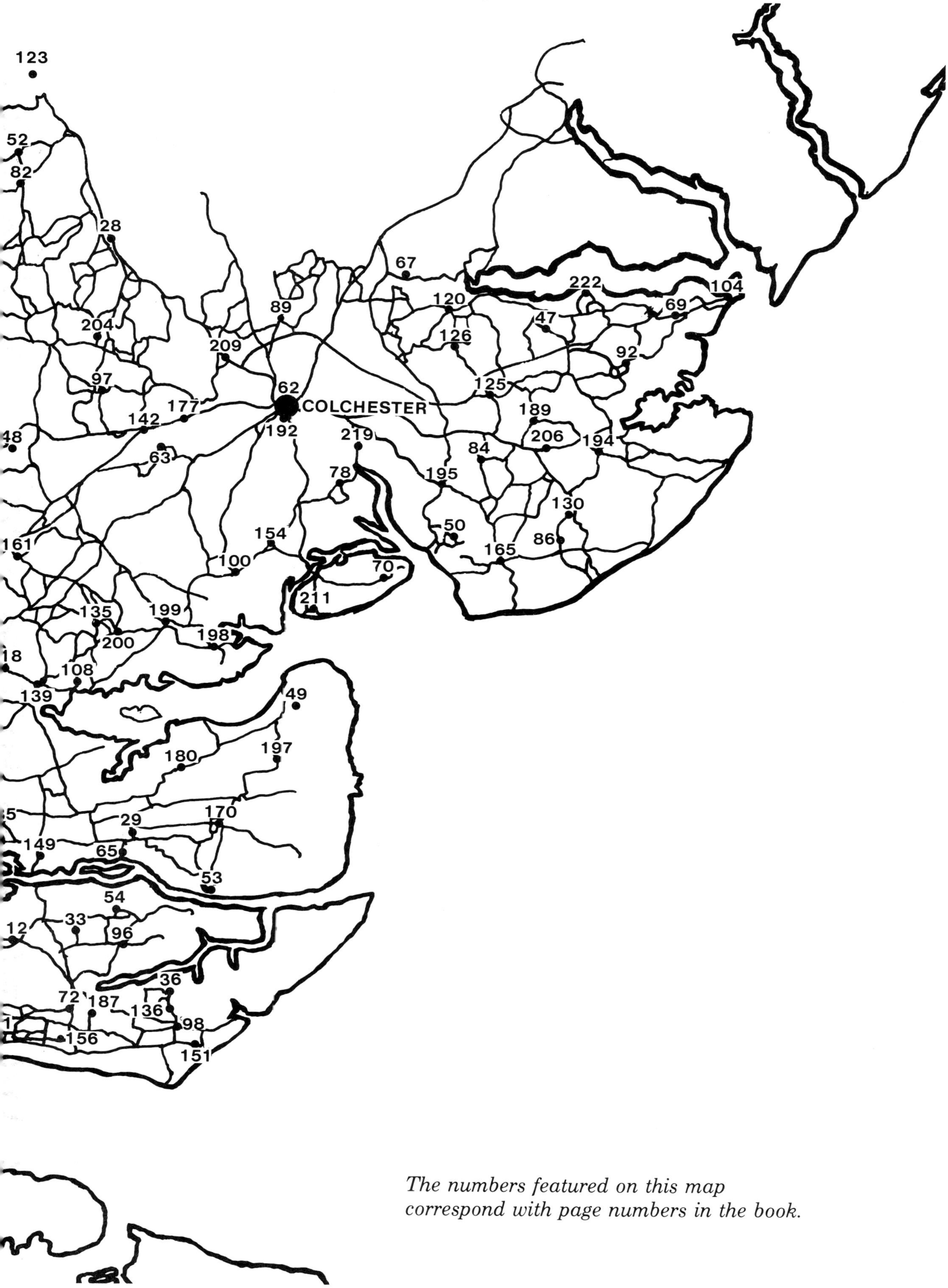

The numbers featured on this map correspond with page numbers in the book.

ACKNOWLEDGEMENT

The author gratefully acknowledges the following subscribers whose support has made the publication of this book possible.

John C. Allen
Society of Antiquaries of London
John S. Appleby
Mrs. M. Arden
Reverend Chris Bard
Barking Central Library
Miss Anne E. Barker
Monica B. Bayley
Michael J. Bellis
Ronald H. Bond
Bookshop Synthese
John H. Boyes
Mrs. E. Burton
P. M. Butler
The Castle Book Shop
Chelmsford Cathedral
Chelmsford County Library
Chelmsford & Essex Museum
Colchester Central Library
Adrian Corder-Birch
Council for the Care of Churches
Peter John Crem
Marcus Dain
University of East Anglia Library
J. C. Emmerson
Essex Archaeological Society
Essex Record Office
University of Essex Library
Leonard H. Farrow
Dr. N. E. Farrow
Brian Myles Foley
J. F. Green
Selwyn Guy
Harlow Museum
J. Hayward
G. E. Holgate
Ilford Central Library
Miss E. M. H. Keary
University of London Library
P. G. Maxey
A. E. McRoberts
David R. Mott
Reverend David Nash
A. S. Newens
Francis A. Newton
Stephen P. Nunn
Parker & Son Ltd
Passmore Edwards Museum
K. N. Paul
R. D. Phillips
Pontifical Institute of Mediaeval Studies – Toronto
Mavis Priestly
C. G. Rosenberg & Company
Royal Academy of Letters Library – Stockholm
Sir John Ruggles-Brise
Aubrey Saunders
David J. Saunders
Harold E. Scarlett
Dudley L. Schrapel
South London Stationers Ltd.
Christopher R. Starr
Martin Stuchfield
C. G. Tait
Robert C. Taylor
Thurrock Local History Museum
Victoria County History of Essex
Victorian Studies Centre
John E. Vigar
Robert James Wager
Ronald Willesden
A. W. Wilson